THIRD EDITION

GRUMPY
IN BELGRADE

CHRIS FARMER

Hundreds miles' away from us but so close to our hearts It's a real pleasure having you as our friends. Thanks for everything.

Love Darko, Natalija & Jelena

Off the wall things that always seem

to happen to me…

Feb-2021.

Author:
Chris Farmer

Publisher:
KOMSHE d.o.o. Beograd

Producer:
Branko Andrić

Editor:
Ivan Kovanović

Illustrations:
Zoran Tovirac Toco

Graphic Design:
Ivan Grujić

Marketing and Sales:
Dimitrije Stamenković
info@komshe.com

For information and distribution
info@komshe.com

Contents

A DAY IN THE LIFE   145

To my dog, Dexter,
because as Mark Twain wrote:
"the more I understand people,
the more I love my dog."

Still Grumpy After All These Years

Preface to the Third Edition

On the occasion of the third edition of *Grumpy in Belgrade,* which hit the bookshelves toward the end of 2014 and continues to hit them up until now, there is one question that I keep asking myself:

Am I still grumpy?

Looking at some of the texts in this volume, some of which were written very early in my time here in Belgrade – what began as a weekend trip has now stretched into an odyssey of 18 years – I begin to realize that I am actually *less* grumpy now than I was when I was younger. Does that make sense?

When I first arrived here, back in 2002, the world I found seemed to be on its head. First of all, I did not understand a word of Serbian; I could not read many of the street signs as they were in Cyrillic script; and every time I did not understand what was happening around me someone would say, "This is Serbia."

This is Serbia indeed. And it goes a lot further to explain my discombobulation than I once thought. This is not to say that Serbia has more strangeness than anywhere else I have lived. I have been in the US (which was strange enough in the 1970s and has become a Trumpian twilight zone today), in Saudi Arabia, in Italy, in France, in the UK (formerly of Europe), in Germany, and in Hong Kong (formerly of the UK) in the course of my life. I have had occasion to see a great deal of strangeness.

And as we all know, strange leads to grumpy.

But this is Serbia. And here, as the years go by, I begin to realize the uniqueness of this country and its people. The stories that you will find in this book are ones that were written by someone who was discovering the culture, the habits, and the customs of a country new to him. Grumpy was maybe the wrong word: dazed and confused might have suited better.

I am still a little dazed and confused, I must admit, as I go through my daily life here in the White City on the Danube. Things continue to baffle and bewilder me. Every time I go into a bookstore, for example, I can find this book in the biography section, the tourism section, the *domaci* author section (!), and once in the cooking section. But then I realize that this is not an easily classified book. There needs to be a section for *Foreign Language Authors in Belgrade Writing About Being Foreign Language Authors in Belgrade.* I don't think that is asking too much…

This is Serbia, and it continues to be Serbia. It is a place full of unexplained mysteries, odd superstitions, and an inexplicable number of fasting days. The longer I live here, the more I realize that I have been bamboozled and befuddled by things that should not be explained. In fact, the further realization is that not only am I confused by Serbia, but I am also at a loss to understand my own country – the same US that I left as a child is not the same.

My conclusion and my resolution, henceforth, is to keep my mouth shut. If I see something I don't understand, I will bury it away. When I am walking my dog and people want to call him, I will take it in stride. When I don't have exact change at the shops, I will give them a few extra dinars to keep the peace. And I have a feeling that the end result of all this good will and silence will be another grumpy book!

Watch this space.

Chris Farmer
February, 2020

ACKNOWLEDGEMENTS

My sincere thanks to everyone who has read this book over the years and has made it the surprising success that it has become. I am truly humbled and honored.

I would like to thank the residents of Belgrade who may find themselves pictured herein and also the ones who do not. Every day is an education to me, and I am grateful to be allowed to learn.

And finally, I thank and commend those of you who have read my words and resisted the urge to punch me in the face.

Thank you all!

MANUFACTURER'S WARNING

NOTICE: The following sequence of words may be harmful to the reader's Normal View of the World.

The manufacturer cannot be held responsible for the contagious effects of "grumpiness" in as much as so much around him seems to inspire it. The manufacturer is not, however, consistently grumpy.

But it seems that he is easily provoked.

This book is a compilation of various blogs and essays by the manufacturer since arriving in Serbia in 2002. A lot of it can be found on his B92 blog, but others have slipped through the cracks in the time-space continuum. These blogs have also been seen in the daily newspaper *Politika* (in Serbian), in *Belgrade New Times* and *Belgrade Life* (may they rest in peace), the website *LivinginBelgrade.com*, the bi-weekly newspaper *Belgrade Insight*, and a few others here and there. Mostly there.

The active ingredients: Irony (92%), Sarcasm (68%), Flippancy (22%), Irreverence (14%), and Indignation (less than 1%). Vitamins OMG and WTF in trace amounts only.

The manufacturer suggests that this combination of active ingredients is highly conducive to creating a picture of the World As He Sees It. To the casual reader, it would seem that he sees it as being a little on its head. The manufacturer advises reading the book upside-down to compensate.

Studies have shown that the manufacturer's view comes from his continued surprise at the way people behave, not only in Serbia but people in general. As it happens, the contents of this book were inspired by his years in Serbia, and some of the references are to unquestionably Serbian phenomena (see "*Speak Warriors*" and "*This is Serbia*").

In general, the manufacturer calls 'em as he sees 'em. Truth, as a subjective additive, is left as optional for the reader to sprinkle on after reading. The manufacturer notes that judgmental ideas of good, bad, right, wrong, truth, or consequences were not part of the original formula and should not be taken in combination with this or any other text.

A long-time (long-term?) resident of Belgrade, the manufacturer brings you this collection hopefully as a means to smile a little at the goings-on of the Serbian capital, its shops, and its roadways. And other stuff.

While every effort has been made to provide you with a safe reading environment, certain combinations of words may provoke ill effects. In this case, dispose of this book in a local incinerator and purchase a new copy immediately.

In case of undesirable effects, stop reading immediately. Wash eyes with a television sitcom, applying liberally as needed until the burning sensation ceases. The manufacturer assures you that this kind of side effect occurs in only 87% of cases.

Thank you.

Chris Farmer,
The Manufacturer

ABOUT THE AUTHOR

When he is not complaining about the minutia of life in the Serbian capital, Chris Farmer has had a number of day jobs. He worked in advertising in London, in sales in Germany, in sports brands in Italy, and in strategic communication in Serbia.

Born in Iowa in the late 1850s, Chris has lived in Dhahran (Saudi Arabia), Rome, Paris, London, Munich, Aixe-en-Provence, Hong Kong, and Perugia before settling in/for Belgrade in 2002.

Graduating with a degree in comparative literature from The American University of Paris, he has spent most of his life in business – confusing clients with quotes from French poetry all the while.

Chris Farmer is the author of a volume of poetry, of innumerable blogs, essays, columns, and one unpublished novel in the back of his closet.

He currently lives in Belgrade, working as a communications consultant and teaching brand management.

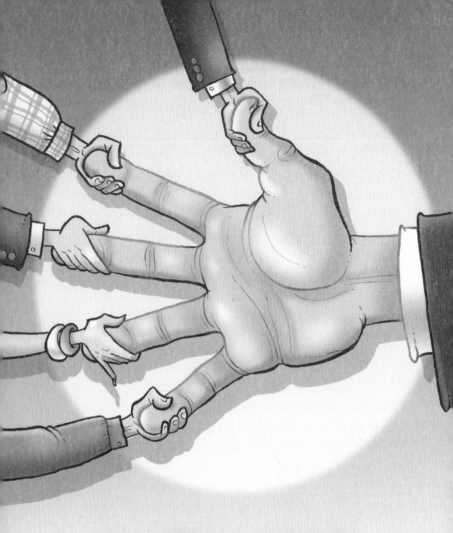

SOCIAL
CONTRACT

SOCIAL
CONTRACT

The stories you are about to read are true. Only the names have been changed to protect the innocent. And some of the facts. And parts of the stories are made up. And some of it never happened.

But the REST is true.

I have long since given up the idea of ever being able to say "Now I've seen everything!" After living here for such a long time, I now EXPECT to see everything.

As a professional foreigner at large on the streets of Belgrade, I end up seeing things that do not register on my Weird-o-Meter. It is not because weird things happen more here than elsewhere, I suppose, but rather that weird things just happen all the time and we casually stroll by them.

In this spirit, when we walk down the street and see someone walking a rhinoceros, a lot of us just step out of the way of his horn and carry on. People like me on the other hand will react, possibly remarking something such as OH MY GOD A RHINOCEROS!

This section (while completely free of rhinos) picks up on the small things which pass as normal in Belgrade. Whether it be the expectation of recovering lost umbrellas, advertising to tourists in code, or stapling animals to the walls of the zoo. It is always the little things that count.

You get used to them. Or you have a psychotic episode.

"This is SERBIA"

While my memory is not the sharpest or the best in the world, I think I can manage to remember where I am. Most of the time anyway.

Still, it never ceases to amaze me how many times, in the course of a normal month, week, day, and (on bad days) hour, people will invoke this sentence as a definitive argument and statement of fact. People will constantly tell me THIS IS SERBIA when I wonder why I cannot figure out the city bus schedule. Why does every official act require a mile-high stack of signed and stamped papers? THIS IS SERBIA! Where is the waiter with my change? THIS IS SERBIA! Why do we repair all the roads at once when the traffic is highest? THIS IS SERBIA!

Ah! Then that's ok.

As a foreigner living here, I suppose it is normal that people should remind me of my physical location every time something happens which baffles and befuddles. Obviously I just don't get it. Obviously things work far differently in Serbia from anywhere else in the world. And obviously I should just shut my mouth and swallow when anyone tells me THIS IS SERBIA – it means that whatever is happening is beyond my comprehension. The thinking man might agree to this if, say, he were landed on an alien planet in the far reaches of the Andromeda Galaxy. In a place where no human habitation has taken root, if someone told me THIS IS ANDROMEDA, I might nod and accept. But as far as most anthropologists can figure, Serbia – like most of Earth – is filled with humans. Maybe I am just naïve to think that humans in Serbia are just the same as humans elsewhere. This is Serbia, after all.

But when things go wrong, or strangely or generally sidewise, the stock explanation that is provided to us (i.e., us foreign guests in this land) is not one which includes a comparison of cultures or values or norms. We get the THIS-IS-SERBIA, and that is meant to explain the whole thing. We are meant to be satisfied with this answer, implying that certain behaviors or practices are simply inexplicable by any other means.

This gives me pause to wonder if, among Serbs, the phrase is also pulled out to explain the unexplainable. Or do they just look at each other and exchange a knowing look that says, "Thank God we do not have to try to tell a foreigner what this means because THIS IS SERBIA and he could never wrap his head around it." I do not like an unsolved mystery. If I am forced to accept that no words, illustrations, or pantomime are available to explain something to me, I will cheerfully rebel. Usually the THIS IS SERBIA is invoked to cover bad situations or problems. Showing up for a residence card renewal and finding that I am missing one important paper that no one told me about, for example. THIS IS SERBIA, they will say, with the implied subtext that I should have KNOWN that something unexpected and illogical would happen.

While THIS IS SERBIA answers the question "What country is this?" adequately and sufficiently, it is not enough to satisfy when faced with unacceptable situations. Moreover, it is not an argument that I, as a foreigner here, can ever use to my own advantage. Once when pulled over for speeding, the policeman asked me how fast I thought I was going. I told him THIS IS SERBIA! But it did not prevent him from writing me up. Maybe this is a magical place in which the laws of physics, civics, and human psychology do not apply. Perhaps I should do a study on the basic differences between Serbia and any other country, but I fear my research would leave me with only one result...

THIS IS SERBIA.

Honestly Speaking

Back from holiday? You got fat.

I never know how to respond to something like that. It seems that people, obsessed as they are with being 'honest' with each other, are happy to tell each other the most outlandishly offensive things in the name of being honest. So they will tell you: you are fat; you look like crap; you are bald; your shoes are ugly; and you smell bad.

And that is on a GOOD day.

Since when is rudeness forgivable under a flag of Honesty? I often hear people say that they are not polite, they are honest with others. Personally, if it seems absolutely necessary to catalogue my faults, shortcomings, and defects by way of a friendly greeting, then I suppose I could accept it. But is it ever really necessary to say these things?

What is the opposite of polite? If we say being honest is its opposite, it means that every time anyone is polite to us, they are lying. This does not seem right. Being polite does not mean telling lies. If I did get fat over the summer, I would not expect someone to tell me that I lost weight. But, on the other hand, I am also quite aware that I got fat – I do not need you (or the others) to inform me of this.

I got fat? Oh God! Why didn't anyone tell me?!?

This is often ascribed here to a Serbian vs. Anglo-Saxon problem. The typical Anglo-Saxon is non-confrontational. He does not want to offend. He speaks more circuitously. If he has a negative comment to make, he hides it inside a question or phrases it without sharp edges. Commonly he makes a joke about himself which might point out some failing on your part. He is not lying to you – he is filtering.

In the meantime, the Serbian way is much more direct. He may want to talk to you about his summer holiday on Halkidiki, about his neighbor's dog, or his views on BusPlus, but first he establishes that he sees you and notices that you are fat. In a way, it's SO obvious to him and everyone else that you got fat, that it would be dishonest NOT to say so. Once that is out of the way, he can get back to the real topic of the conversation.

This is also true when it comes to simple yes or no questions. I am still left speechless when, upon walking to a Belgrade shop and asking for some product, they just say "Nema." It is direct. It is factual (usually). And it is verbally economic. No excuses are made. No promises of getting new supplies next Tuesday. Just plain No.

The explanation, the reason why something is not there, or the fact that some will be there soon, or that we have many similar products which you might like are all forms of politeness. As a consumer, I like that kind of politeness. Compare:

- Do you have any shoelaces?
- I am sorry but we don't have any right now. You might try Wilson's next door or pop in later in the week. We should be getting more by then.
- Do you have any shoelaces?
- No.
- You have nothing else to tell me?
- You are fat.

When politeness is a lie and honesty is the ability to say every rude thing you can think of, then the rules of conversation such as I learned them are upside-down. Please, if I should accidentally say something that does not offend you, insult you, or bruise your ego, then you must understand. It is because I am a liar.

Mind your Manners, Please.

As a child, I got my hands slapped quite often.

I would forget to say please (slap). I would omit to say thank you (slap again).I would sometimes burst into a room whose door was closed without knocking (slap-slap). And thus I was taught what everyone in America of the late sixties and seventies, my formative years one might say, called "good manners" and "being polite." After several million slaps, I actually started to get it.

Everything got easier after I finally learned this lesson. People listened to me more. My parents smiled more. I got a few more birthday and Christmas gifts. I heard people say – My what a GOOD boy. What a POLITE boy. This had been working for me until I left America. Then things started to get more complicated...

The idea of being polite was driven by the idea of showing respect for the person to whom you are talking. Not a respect like student to Maharishi or loyal subject to the Queen, but rather it was a base level of interchange in conversation which smoothed over rough edges. By saying please, thank you, and you're welcome, you demonstrate that you respect the other person enough to be aware of their sensibilities. It does not matter if I had to learn it by rote – the idea of civility and politeness also sunk in.

Then I arrived in Belgrade.

Politeness here is not unknown. The Serbian language contains all of the structures and forms for exceedingly polite conversation. But it is not used in the same way, at the same times, or with the same people as in American English. In familiar circles, with friends or family, the idea of politeness is treated with suspicion. It is seen as being fake or artificial, unnecessary and sometimes even offensive.

It is common enough to use the imperative tense without modifying your commands – Give me that! Close the door! Come here! In all of these examples, I would (mistakenly) say "please" by way of softening the command. The subtext is something like:

"It-is-not-myplace-or-station-to-issue-orders-to-you-but-I-would-be-very-grateful-if-you-could-close-the-door.   Please." More and more I begin to think that this reflects a certain insecurity in Anglo-Saxon native speakers. We are uncertain, perhaps, that our good intentions or feelings are understood. So we have to put words around them.

This is also representative of an economy of language which we do not have in English. In Serbian, we do not waste time with the amenities and niceties of the pleases and the thank yous. They are understood. They are implicit. Why say something that needs no saying? Maybe that is why we do not even modify our nouns in Serbian – no definite or indefinite articles please, we have already said enough.

Habit being what it is, I continue to say thank you to everyone. The merchant, the waiter, the friend, the child, the doctor, and anyone with whom I end up talking. Even the cop giving me a parking ticket gets a polite thank you as I turn to speed away from him.

On other occasions, people have got angry with me (or at least what I perceive as anger when voices are raised) for insisting on my idea of politeness. I do not like people walking into my office unannounced – I need them to knock on the door. They don't of course. And now to all of you who are about to tell me how useless it is for me to dedicate a whole column to this meaningless talk I have only one thing to say:

Thank you very much.

Drive-by Wavers

When someone speeds down the middle of Branko's Bridge, weaving and swerving at 130 kph, he might throw you a polite wave. As if to say, "Sorry to have caused you a near-death experience."

When a driver struggles and attempts to parallel park five times on a busy Belgrade street, he may also wave to the accumulated traffic. As if to say, "Thanks for being patient and not killing me." How we drive, then, is a reflection of how we live in the society composed of the impolite, the rude, the aggressive, the dangerous, and the frightening. Most of the time, these five elements bring the rest of us down to their level.

I discovered this recently when I was attempting to explain to my newly motorized fiancée exactly why she should wave an excuse to the car behind her when she stalled at the traffic light on Cvijićeva. As a point of principle, she need not have acknowledged anything. She could have restarted the car and proceeded as planned, which in fact she did.

And I realized that she was right.

I really wanted her to wave as a way to ward off trouble. My experience with traffic in Belgrade has brought me to the conclusion that people are complete lunatics when they get behind the wheel. I expect them to draw their weapons and raise their fists at the slightest provocation. If it had been ME, I certainly would have waved – not because I thought I was in the wrong but because I did not want to buy myself any trouble. That is precisely how I explained it – demonstrating that I am completely ready to compromise my values and principles in order to avoid problems and, eventually, violence.

I still think the urge to avoid violence is a good and useful instinct. But I am questioning now how what we do perpetuates our systemic bowing to it. "Appeasement," by the way, turned out to be a very stupid strategy for Neville Chamberlain as he watched Hitler march into Poland in 1939.

On the other hand, how can we – individual citizens – expect to change society by refusing to give into its warped set of values? How does refusing to give your doctor a bottle of whiskey protect you from getting bad treatment or (more likely) NO treatment at all? How does not accepting incompetence from a shop clerk make your shopping experience any better? How does complaining at ill-treatment get you anything more than additional ill-treatment?

And why should I apologize to a speeding driver just because I might be going slower than he?

The more we appease the rude, the impolite, the aggressive, the dangerous, and the frightening, the more of their 'qualities' we can expect to endure. Now that I have said this out loud, I am faced with the choice of how I will implement this discovery in my daily life. I will probably continue to proffer perfunctory apologies, even when they are underserved, out of habit.

If you cut me off in traffic, your wave will not get you any extra points. If you are driving slowly, however, I might not now honk my horn so quickly. Living in a society that promotes habitual bad behavior based mostly on fear is not my idea of the Good Life.

But habits and routines and ritual compromises, like traffic lights, inevitably change.

Umbrellas and the Nature of Civic Responsibility

PRACTICAL TIP: In a yes or no question, the answer is almost never "it's not my ice cream."

Had I known that, I probably would not have experienced this afternoon's cerebral implosion. As it happens, I walked up to the kiosk and asked my question, anticipating a no, hoping for a yes. And that is what I got.

The backstory is equally ridiculous, but that is entirely my fault. Yesterday, sensing rain, I went out into the streets armed with my umbrella. An umbrella, as we all know, very nearly qualifies as public property. If you leave it someplace, it is no longer yours but passes into the public domain on the basis of need. This having been said, I was somewhat attached to this particular umbrella. I had kept it for at least eight months without losing it. It was the right size and worked well. For the past months, it has served as my principle umbrella while the primary and secondary backups remained in the trunk of my car.

I stopped by the kiosk on Trg Republika to take out my hat and gloves, and, in so doing, hooked my umbrella on the adjacent ice cream stand. I then walked away without my umbrella – realizing the omission only eight bus stops later. My point is that I did not actually lose the umbrella, but I abandoned it.

Thinking today that I might try to see if some kindly soul had kept the abandoned umbrella for me, I stopped by the kiosk to ask if it had been found. Hence the yes or no question. I asked the woman nicely, noting that I had left it by accident on her ice cream wagon.

"It's not my ice cream."

"Yes, but –" I tried to clarify that it could be the Pope's ice cream and it would not matter to my question.

"What do you want?"

"I left my – "

"It's not my ice cream."

This is a classic Schrödinger's Cat scenario wherein the answer, ensconced inside her head, could be simultaneously both yes and no. I will never know if she found my umbrella and gave it to her nephew Vuk who went out yesterday without one and ran the risk of catching a cold. Or not. She flatly refused to answer my question, but she opened up a larger one.

Her response meant to me that she wanted a dialogue on the Nature of Civic Responsibility. In this dialectic, I already had three strikes against me: a) I was stupid enough to leave it there; b) it is not her ice cream and therefore does not behoove her to feel responsible for items left thereupon, c) and I was naïve enough to come back and ask about it.

The interesting part to me is the circuitous route which led her from my question to her neighbor's ice cream. I asked about an umbrella. She heard me accusing her of having an ice cream wagon. From having the wagon, she moved quickly along to whose responsibility it might be for the wagon, and who should answer questions about it, and how could I possibly think that she might be answerable to its inadvertent contents (i.e., my umbrella). And, therefore: "It's not my ice cream."

QED.

She could have said, as people are very fond of doing here, "no." I would have been slightly disappointed but unsurprised. But in denying ownership of the ice cream, she managed to make me both slightly disappointed AND surprised.

Tomorrow, with my primary backup umbrella in hand, I will stop by again and ask to buy an ice cream from her.

The Good Jeans

I have recently discovered that all jeans are not created equally.

First there are the Guy Jeans. The Guy Jeans are selected for the criteria of comfort, price, and convenience. No other factors are available for Guy Jeans and the better deal you can get and the faster you can be in and out of the shop with your jeans, the higher your score.

Needing a new pair of jeans recently, I set out to shops and browsed a little (i.e., 25 minutes). I then took myself to buvlijak to see what the fake market had. I found two pairs of "Levis" (the quotes are meant to indicate that no similarities exist between actual Levis and the ones I found) for €20. And I found them in record time! And they fit fine and were comfortable enough! I thought I had made the score of the century and promptly and proudly brought them home.

But I was wrong.

This leads us to the second category of jeans. This one accounts for things like style, and cut, and boot legs, straight legs, high waist, low waist, distinctive colors, and many other criteria which were heretofore absent in my jeans shopping. These would be Good Jeans (diametrically opposed to Guy Jeans except by accident).

Good Jeans, as judged by the Self-Appointed Arbiter of Taste and Aesthetics (i.e., my girlfriend) have almost NOTHING in common with the good deal which I thought I had made at the flea market. Good Jeans required time to choose. They are on average ten times more expensive. They do not have to be comfortable.

And functionality is only a side-benefit of Good Jeans.

Now that I own a pair of these Good Jeans (and my Guy Jeans of which I had been so proud are now secretly hidden at the bottom of a closet underneath other unsuitable clothes), I can begin to see the point. They do look better (one supposes) than the ones I chose myself. But I freely admit that I am hard pressed to see the difference. Having always bought Guy Jeans and prized their functionality as the supreme criterion, it has become part of my education to learn to perceive the subtle differences.

One vital qualification of Good Jeans that set them apart from my Guy Jeans – and one which I have sorely overlooked for nearly half a century – is what she thinks of them. And since she likes them, then they are Right.

The Guy Jeans will remain in hiding.

Cats and Dogs

When a cat jumps up on a shelf and knocks over a glass vase, she tends to sit there and pretend that she had nothing to do with the noise and mess. Confront the cat, and she will give you the Look. If it is a dog that bounds into a room and breaks the vase, he will immediately cower and whimper and look extremely guilty.

Does this sound familiar to anyone?

In the relationship between men and women, men will always be the dogs. We are simple. We make a lot of messes. We break things. We bark when we are upset. We hide when we are afraid. The veneer of the Big Mean Dog is only that – window dressing.

And if the men are dogs, the women are the complicated, slinking, seductive, and unaffected felines. I have resisted this idea for a very long time, thinking it was too much of a generalization, a stereotype. But then the proof always comes back to slap me on the muzzle. "Bad dog," the proof says sternly.

Entering a house, for example. When a cat enters the house, she walks around and looks at things. She touches your books. She wants to see all the rooms (even the bathroom that you forgot to clean). She takes possession of the space before settling down on the sofa. When a dog comes in, however, he looks for something to chew. He stays by your feet. He wants to play with you – NOW. He is not interested in your collection of dolls, your choice of magazines or dish washing soap. He never finds out if you even HAVE a bathroom.

Another key thing which echoes in relationships is that dogs have definite owners. If he is your dog, he listens to you, he comes when you call, he is happy to see you when you come home from work. Cats, on the other hand, are the owners. A cat will wait until you come to her to stroke her. She might let you pick her up, but then struggle to get away in a few minutes.

If you are reading, she will come between you and the book. When you come home from work, the cat is always too busy to come see you.

In the next few weeks, I will be settling into a clearly marked cat space. There are many vases to knock over. There are many shoes to chew. My job (as a simple and messy dog) will be to become much more catlike. But if I come in and try to take over, I will not be rewarded with any pats on the head. The challenge then is to tone down the Dog so the cat does not feel she is being invaded. That should reap rewards!

"Goooood dog."

Surrendering to the Inevitable

This is terrible.

As much as the city is being held in the grip of Nature and the adamantine grip of her snow, so do I – after having resisted for several days – feel inexorably pulled into the Snow Trap. I have to write about the snow. I do not WANT to write about the snow! I rebel against its banality in subject matter! I push against its encroaching walls!

Yet here we are....

I peruse the media, online and off, and find story after story after anecdote after amusing reflection on the snow. We are fascinated and terrified by it. We cancel everything as a result of it. We revel in it and we are repelled by it.

There seem to be no half-measures concerning the snow. It affronts us and demands that we strike up an attitude toward it. Moving from place to place, our footfalls are gripped by it. Travelling by automotive contrivance, we have to spend hours clearing the carcass and breathing life back into it. And the snow keeps falling, keeps covering it back up, and we keep sweeping it away.

Nature always wins.

And there are the enviably free spirits who embrace the snow. They run out into it. They jump. They play. They make snow angels and expose themselves to frostbite without care. They make snowmen who smell through carrots and see through small stones. They laugh a lot and they smile a lot. I like them. They are not oppressed by the white blanket. They are nurtured by it.

Most of us grumble, however. We stomp and grumble to the shops. We shake and shiver and wish we were back indoors. We wonder why-in-the-name-of-God we came out in the first place. Usually we did not leave our homes in the name of God, but in the name of Carrying On Regardless.

We like to think that we are somehow more than mere Nature. It is only snow, after all. It is just a thing in our way, we think. But it stymies us. Impossible as it is to pretend it is not an obstacle, we pretend all the same. Trudging and slipping and getting up and pressing on, we arrive at our destination and what then do we do?

We talk about the snow.

Herding and Pasturing

The scene in the Sava Centar parking lot should have told me everything.

Having been told to meet our bus in this parking lot to begin the 12-hour trip to Halkidiki, we duly showed up at the appointed time and place. Instead of seeing our bus, however, we saw at least 20 such conveyances, surrounded with hundreds of bag-laden holidaymakers.

The process of transformation had already begun.

The cacophony of voices, calling to each other, crying children, screaming parents, laughing youth, and assorted conversational counterpoints, had already begun to meld together into a collective kind of lowing and mooing. The crowds began slowly to be herded into their various corrals, moving with a kind of unfocused cud-chewing determination, offering the occasional disgruntled "moo" when prodded by any of the herders (i.e., Tour Leaders).

We, the large domesticated ungulates, having renounced our humanity for the sake of a cheap getaway to the Aegean Sea, were now branded and rounded up into the different buses. Slotted into our stalls, the bus slowly rolled off into the horizon.

We spent a few hours uncomfortably in our stalls, occasionally grazing on the feedbags we all prepared while we were still humanoids – at the sound of the first sandwich being unwrapped, the entire herd broke out the food, and the sound of elliptical chewing pervaded the bus, drowning out the music leaking out of the speakers.

When from time to time we were released from our captivity, the movement of the herd was in the predictable pattern. Left to our own devices, the cows spread out from the door of the bus over a wide area, but soon the herd was drawn back together near the door. Stamping our feet against the cold in the night; hiding from the sunlight in the shade of the bus during the day.

As cattle go, we were a very well behaved herd. Back on the bus, we received instructions as to how to telephone (and the herd complied), where and what to eat (and the cows complied), and what to look at (this met with mixed success – we are cows after all).

Upon arrival for pasturing in Halkidiki (which is the Greek word for land-inhabited-by-vacationing-Serbs), some of us reverted in due course to human form. Others, however, maintained the integrity of the herd and moved together in small groups, looking for places to graze, protecting the young in their circles, and mooing in distinctively Serbian tones. When a few got separated from the others, they would begin their bovine vocalizations in order to reconstitute the herd. Cows are generally social creatures and enjoy each others' company. Mini-corrals were organized for short range cattle drives to various new pastures, and the lowing ranks held. The cowpokes could be proud of their livestock.

Finally, after a few days, the process went into reverse and we were led from our temporary stables back to the comfort of the bus-stalls. It was apparent from the first that the social structure of the herd had been changed somewhat, with certain breeds and families choosing to intermingle.

The herding and pasturing was complete. Many of us returned to our lives without even realizing that the bovine transformation ever took place. But others, in terrifying awareness, knew it all too well. The experience, for the uninitiated, can be traumatizing. Next year I will certainly give thought to joining a flock of birds instead.

Of Women and Men's Rooms

This is the trouble with crowd sourcing.

I have been asked to write about the relationship between men and women. In order to do so, I am forced to call upon my many years experience as a male and attempt to relate the relative truths and gleanings from this experience into a form which will elucidate and provide the invaluable insight which this topic requires and deserves. The effort has been extreme, but I finally believe that I might impart this wisdom – the sum total of my understanding of the relationship between women and men.

"?"

This having been said, I do know a thing or two about women in the men's room. I know, for example, that they are not supposed to be there. One day last week, however, I had occasion to visit three different men's rooms in three different public places. And each time, there was a woman there.

Hm… I hmmed to myself.

In the prudish primitive culture from which I sprang, it was generally thought of as unthinkable to have a woman in the men's room. It is an unwritten rule – no one having bothered to write it down because it would appear self-evident. If we posit the existence of separate lavatories for men and women, it is presupposed that each sex would repair to their respective doors, willingly and devoid of argument.

The women in the men's room this week were not patrons (note the gender-specific term), but they were there cleaning. One agrees with cleaning the lavatories. One does not object to their being as hygienic as possible. One does not even object too strongly to the overpowering ammoniac smell of the disinfectant. But one (i.e., this one, i.e., me) does NOT expect to see the cleaning going on while one is going about one's bathroomly business. One expects to wait rather uncomfortably and impatiently in the corridor in front of a sign that says something like closed for maintenance or closed for cleaning or closed-due-to-the-presence-of-females-in-what-is-traditional-ly-a-space-reserved-for-males,   the-Last-Bastion-of-sanctioned-segregation.

That would be a complicated sign however.

In all three cases last week, the women carried on regardless with their duties. Cleaning and straightening while the toilet was being trafficked by several men. I note, further, that no one except me seemed to think this was strange or somehow unusual. Not wanting to make a scene, I pretended that I was cool with this turn of events. And I admit that this was far from the first time this has captured my attention in the ten years I have been in Serbia. But it happened three times that day. When things occur in threes, it MUST mean something…

So there they were, minding their own business and probably at least a little of our business. The thought then scurried across my mind as to what would happen if it were reversed. Putting the shoe on the other foot, a man cleaning a ladies' room in the presence of women would likely result in a police action.

Let's just call this an Observation and move on, I think. See you around the urinal.

Drunk and Disorderly

There is nothing more sobering than being pulled over for walking under the influence.

According to the brain scientists and rocket surgeons whom we have elected to public office in Belgrade ("we" being loosely applied here), it is NOT enough to switch off the music early. It is NOT enough to close the bars, cafes, and restaurants by midnight. It is NOT enough to curtail the sale of alcohol after a certain hour. Now, if we have a few too many, we will have to sleep in the bars until morning.

Drunk driving is a serious business and should well be down-upon cracked. But the next stumbling steps seem a bit draconian. The intoxicated are banned from public transport. And the drunken staggers which mark many a weekend evening in the White City are now against the law and punishable by fines of up to EUR 3,000.

In practical terms: if you have had too much and have the presence of mind to leave your car behind, you could still be nicked for drunk and disorderly as you walk home. The implications, however, are more staggering still. The implied intent is to get people to drink less. A good thing? Certainly. Another implied result is to force people who DO choose to inebriate themselves to take taxis, all other options being closed to them. Collusion and conspiracy? Possibly. A further implication is in the bulging coffers of the city drunk tank (do we have one?) when the police sweep up a few hundred tipsy citizens winding their way back from an evening on the town. Money spinner? For sure!

Looking at it from the other side, one can see the benefit to the Regular Guy of not having to suffer drunks sitting next to them on the bus. One could also see the advantage of keeping people off the streets who use them as crawl spaces, urinals, vomitoriums, and dance halls owing to the influence of strong drink. Surely that kind of behavior is to be frowned upon.

There is a little civil liberties issue lurking in the back of my head, however. The basic idea is how much the citizen should be responsible for his own actions and how much should be within the purview of the constabulary. We humans regularly choose boneheaded courses of action. We are distinguished from lower animals by that very ability to act stupidly. Does that mean we should embrace our idiot natures and exercise our boneheadedness to the full? No – that is not the question here. The question is this: Are we able, as a species and as citizens within a social structure, to be self-regulating?

And if the laws regulating that social structure appear to be arbitrary, inconsistently applied, or haphazard, how much can the citizen be blamed for being unable to walk the straight line? Big questions, to be sure.

All of this would seem to be a defense of drunkenness. It is not. It is rather a call for a little common sense. Common sense holds that everyone, no matter how unevolved, knows that alcohol impairs the common senses. We also know that smoking is bad for us. We know we should not walk out into the middle of a busy street. We know a lot of things. Making them illegal, however, lifts the responsibility from our shoulders and places it in the hands of the police.

The Solution, therefore, is to finish the job. Let's make the sale and consumption of alcohol illegal. Let's ban cigarettes. Let's furthermore restrict citizens from going from place to place without a specific reason. Let's prevent them from eating too much. Let's ban music. After all, it would seem that we cannot be trusted to eat, drink, move about, or converse without running afoul of the law anyway. With all of us under a kind of general house arrest, the citizen could be sure to be safe and peaceful.

What a beautiful world this would be!

Dunbar's Number

According to what I could discover (and I am sure there is some overly-befriended Facebooker out there who may correct me) the maximum amount of friends you can have on Facebook is five thousand. Five thousand fellow humans whom we call our friends.

5,000? Really?

Scrolling through the ever-changing Facebook interface, one sees people with extraordinarily high friend counts. Personally, I have only seen one with more than 2,000, but I am willing to accept that at least one user (if not many more) has pushed the envelope to its furthest extreme.

Ask most people in the real (i.e., geological) world how many friends they have and they will usually pitch relatively low numbers at you. They will say something like, "Of TRUE friends, only a few." I think we have all heard this before; and a lot of us may have also said this. I have.

But only to my five thousand closest friends.

We want to show our values vis-à-vis friendship. We do not want to be known as people who casually (or frenetically as I have witnessed) go around adding hundreds of friends at random. We will say that our GOOD friends are people who know us well, who we trust. It therefore must be a small number in order to safeguard one's dignity.

But then walks in British anthropologist Robin Dunbar. His 1992 study, using primates who gather into groups of friends to pick lice out of each other's hair, came up with an extrapolated figure for the maximum amount of friends with whom humans can maintain a social relationship. Dunbar's number is 148.

This means that we limited humans cannot know each member, and how each member reacts with each other, in a group greater than 148. Apparently, beyond this number the neocortex starts smoking and setting off alarm bells. My "friend" list on Facebook is just under three hundred. That means about 152 of you are not being processed.

Sorry guys.

The question, as my enquiring friend Simon posed it recently, is about the criteria we set for calling someone a friend. Have they changed? Are we generally less picky than once we were? Do we feel so much more evolved as to be able to stretch our neocortices to the point of bursting? Or is it that the term friend has become outmoded and useless, like the word 'nice'? Nice, by the way, derives from the Latin word nescius, meaning ignorant, foolish, or silly.

Cynic that I usually am, I tend to think that we have just become a little heavy-handed and glib with the appellation of friend. There may be 300 people, or even 3,000, that I like or have met and with whom I have been favorably impressed, but I would be hard put to hang the label of friend around their necks. Firstly, how many of those 3,000 even remember me? Can they be MY friends if I am not theirs? Friendship is usually more of a two-way street, I fancy.

But on Facebook, we can ALL be friends! It is a merry little solipsistic utopia in which anyone whose post I have liked might instantly become my friend. Since this is absurd, I think we need an evolutionarily advanced term for this new breed of friends. Rather than calling them "friends," for example, we should say they are "People In a Network Having Evolved Anthropological Dimensions."

PINHEADs.

This much more descriptive acronym could suffice to cover the extra 152 people in my list and the 4,852 extra PINHEADs on the envelope-pusher's list.

Popping Twinkies

It is insidious. It is erosive. It is pervasive.

I find myself thinking in quips and quotes and bons mots. I am unable to sustain a thought for more than about three seconds before looking for new sensory inputs. I am deathly afraid that I may lose my train of thought and not even be able to finish this blog post. I might substitute a YouTube video instead. I might just encapsulate the whole thing in a three word sentence.

Facebook is slowly robbing me of my already challenged attention span.

Think of one's typical Facebook behavior. You log on. You check what anyone said about your posts. You check a half a dozen other posts. Or a hundred. Each check takes about two to three seconds. You may find something to "Like" and even to read. You scan it. And you move on. Next!

I notice that my sentences are even getting shorter. No more dependent clauses, fewer parenthetical asides, less waxing adjectival. The reasons we are cropping ourselves seem to be two-fold. Firstly, there is an awareness that people will generally not spend the time on longer posts. They will see a clump of words and tell themselves, "I will read this later." But later may never come as the timeline keeps dumping more Stuff to read in front of us. Secondly, and admittedly Facebook was not set up to be a forum for long-winded essayists, there is a premium on Facebook for the aphorism, for crunching complex thoughts into Dorothy-Parkerisms. The net effect is that we believe we are being deeper and profounder than the average bear.

There are a few types of users. There is News Guy. News Guy shares and reposts articles from everything he is reading and, often, does not share any opinion about it. He reads, he likes, and he posts. News Guy might never share an original thought of his own. Then you have Music Guy. Music Guy posts the songs he happens to be listening to at the time. Some people only post their meals. Some post only pictures of their children. Some tell you the minutia of their daily lives. But in all cases, they are just snapshots. We present synecdochic evidence of the greater whole, implying that the tidbit we 'share' is but the tip of the iceberg.

The iceberg cannot be shared.

I have tried to combine all these user-types into my posting. But I cannot escape the common denominator of their brevity and thus their affront to the attention span. Maybe it is just me, but I think that Facebook calls for this kind of usage and fosters it. After time, we get better at the short focus. The process is thus self-perpetuating. I have only been using the platform for about four or five months, but I feel its effects.

Compare, if you will, a beautifully orchestrated five-course gourmet meal and snack food. When we sit down to the meal, whose various courses have been designed to complement each other, to lead naturally along a path of gastronomic delight, culminating in a feeling of satisfaction, we are engaging in a process which requires our whole minds as well as bodies. If, however, we have spent the day popping Twinkies and their incumbent instant gratification, we will not have the wherewithal to sit through the carefully planned meal.

Speaking to the House of Lords in England, among whose ranks Facebook users are few and far between I should imagine, Susan Adele Baroness Greenfield, an Oxford professor of synaptic pharmacology, says the experiences of social networking sites "are devoid of cohesive narrative and long-term significance. As a consequence, the mid-21st century mind might almost be infantilised, characterised by short attention spans, sensationalism, inability to empathise and a shaky sense of identity."

Perhaps this movement toward sound-biting and quipping is a good thing. Maybe the natural course of evolution will see mankind as less of a social animal and more of a socially-networked creature. Perhaps human relationships are not what they used to be. After all, our basic social structure and strictures have been in loosening mode for centuries. This could be the obvious next step.

For what it is worth, I do not think I can forgo the pleasure of the long, protected rant in favor of verbal Twinkies. I am sure they will eventually give me an ulcer.

Extending and Distending

The way I used to calculate it, at Christmas we usually got ONE day off. At New Year's we would also get ONE day to recover. Then it was immediately back to work, back to the office, back to normal. Not so in Serbia.

The Great Holiday exodus began this year about one week before the New Year. After December 26, the answering machines and auto-responders began to take over. The unanswered calls began to increase. The call backs are just starting now, twenty three days later.

For twenty three days, the swell of the twin (or, if you count both East and West, quadruple) winter holidays has been extending and distending like stellar gas after the Big Bang. Even this week, the extension continues as people, while they may be back to work, are spending time catching up for the many days and weeks they have been away. Call again on Monday.

Of course this is both a sign for worry and for relief. The worry comes from the fact that businesses are not getting back to business for such a long time that the approach of the Great July-August Shut Downs suddenly do not seem so far away – only five months to go. And in the middle we will have a mini-hiatus in February where people will go skiing or tell people that they are going skiing. Then we will have the month of May in which, under sunny skies, we prefer to be in sidewalk cafes than in the office and tend to pad out the May Day – Easter Holidays by several days in either direction. This year Good Friday is on April 22, followed by an intervening week, and then it is the May 1 and 2 holidays. Doing the math, that is another twelve days. Hence my worry: when will we be working at all?

The relief, however, is also palpable. If everyone feels that it is ok to take off half the year (not counting weekends) in public/private holidays, then it must mean the economy is strong enough to withstand it. Doesn't it? It must mean that companies and businesses need not worry about any lack of productivity. It must mean that no decisions are really urgent aside from which mountain, which beach, or which family home will be chosen for the other half of the year.

Maybe it would be easier just to declare December, January, May, July, and August (plus a few pieces of February, April, and September) as being Closed for Business. That still gives us six months to get on with things, doesn't it?

AUTO-RESPONDER: We are sorry but we are out of the office most of the time. Please leave a message and you will be contacted within 45 days. Thank you.

Oh yeah. Thanks.

Thanksgiving is a survivor holiday.

The pilgrims were happy and thankful in 1637 that America had not killed them all. The Indians were happy and thankful that the pilgrims had not killed them all (yet). They survived. As a tribute to their survival, Americans traditionally eat themselves into oblivion on this holiday.

And not everyone will survive.

I was reminded about half way through this day that today is Thanksgiving Day in America. Somehow I had forgotten what is arguably one of the most celebrated holidays back home. I was reminded about it not by a fellow American but by a Bulgarian.

With only a few hours left of Thanksgiving, it would behoove me to express my gratitude quickly – all the quicker to get back to my standard cynical posture tomorrow.

However, unlike the pilgrims, I am casting around now for things to be thankful for – aside from those immutables like family and friends, health and soundness of mind (on most days). The pilgrims were grateful for a negative: they were happy they did not die. I suppose I am happy for this too. In those terms, one may be happy for a lot of things:

- I am thankful that I did not get hit by the bus which grazed the brim of my cap while walking home today.

- I am grateful that despite the prodigious quantity consumed, I never choked on any ćevapi or the attendant cabbage.

- I am grateful that the new smoking law does not reach its influence into my home.

- I am grateful and happy that no one ever calls on me to say too many polysyllabic words in Serbian.

- I am thankful that many shops have not had much milk or cheese for the past few weeks, helping me stick to my diet.

- I am thankful that there is nothing good on television in the afternoons.

- I am thankful for the return of freezing weather, lest my gloves never be used this year.

- I am thankful for merchants and shopkeepers who do not waste their time talking to me more than absolutely necessary to tell me they do not have what I want. "Nema."

- I am thankful not to have suffered a cardiac infarction on the treadmill by trying to keep up with the Serious Gym Guys.

- I am thankful for Velcro, because, well… who isn't?

If I had remembered the holiday, I might have had a much longer list of those terrible and unspeakable things which failed to happen to me this year for which I am infinitely thankful.

And this is something for which YOU can be thankful.

Fighting Words

What makes us want to punch each other?

This morning, leaving my home, there was a guy who wanted to take my parking space. But he decided to wait for it in such a way as I could not easily get out of it. I signaled him to move and he inched away - it was enough for me to pass but I had to do six maneuvers to get by without hitting him.

I signaled again for him to move. This time the response was to open the window and ask me angrily what I wanted. The position he chose was immediately aggressive. He was ready to fight. I declined.

A couple of weeks ago, I witnessed a man who came looking for a fight with someone out of Heroism: he came to defend the honor of his girlfriend. But instead of letting his words talk, he moved immediately to violence. A fight ensued. Blood was drawn. The police were called.

We are aggressive people. The incident above did not involve me, but I have felt the same kind of rage from time to time in my life. Many have. But the question I have is when does it become acceptable to cross the line between civilized behavior, even if angry, and unchecked violence and aggression?

If you watch television or films, or (and perhaps worse still) television films, you are likely to see several people being punched in the face or fighting in the course of a day. When I was younger, I remember that it always the Bad Guy who did the punching and the Good Guy would defend himself.

And he would usually win.

But in today's imagery, we are more likely to see the perceived Good Guy lose his temper and start the fight. We are being trained and conditioned to react violently and aggressively. If not, we are seen as cowardly or as weak.

I teach my son to avoid fights in school. I try to show him that words are just as effective. That people who want to resort to shoving matches are the ones who have run out of words to say what they feel, to control themselves, and to solve their own problems. I do not mean, by this, that he should be the quickest and cleverest in doing the dozens. I don't think having the better (or louder) insult ready is the solution. I want him to disarm aggression before it becomes violent.

Have I, in counseling this, left him an easy target to school bullies?

This is my greatest fear. The fact is that aggression has become an acceptable standard. Begin talking about violence and aggression and you will soon find everyone around you has a few stories - some of them will be understandable, some will turn your insides out.

Most people who get into fights will protest that they had no choice or that it was not their fault. These are rationalizations. We do not always like the choices, but we always have them. And a real fight involves at least two participants: how can we not take our own share of the responsibility? But we offer these rationalizations, I think, because we secretly know that resorting to violence is a failure of civilized behavior.

Even if it is glamorized in the movies.

Suspension and Bridges

What we need in Belgrade, really, is a suspension bridge.

We need a bridge that will suspend our doubts about ever having enough viable bridges. We need a bridge that will suspend our disbelief about the dangers of travelling over the Gazela Bridge.

After the early reports of the damage to the pylons holding Gazela above the water's surface, I immediately had a picture in my mind of cars and trucks driving merrily into a gaping hole and over the edge to pile up in the Sava. Lemming-like, on the second day after the announcement, I was driving to New Belgrade behind a huge line of cars to cross this bridge. Given the option of driving through town, adding an extra hour at least to the crossing, and risking it all to use the bridge, I chose the latter. I consulted my passengers and they sided with me. We chose the danger.

Suspension of disbelief.

The news of the damaged pylons made me think of the dramatic bridge collapse in Minneapolis, Minnesota two years ago which claimed the lives of 13 and injured many more. In the meantime, Belgrade city authorities keep telling us it is safe to use and will be fixed in 15 days. They neglected to tell us when the 15 days would start…

For years there have been calls for more bridges and plans to renovate the Gazela Bridge. It was supposed to start two years ago, then last year, then this summer, and now – given the pressing need – sometime adjacent to now. The works have been delayed and delayed. The last mayoral race in Belgrade was run partially on the amount of time it would take to build a new bridge over Ada (2 years? 3 years? 4 years?).

With the new traffic law in place, forcing motorists to attach bluetooth devices to their ears that look like Borg implants, the next step was only logical. The strategy has been to wait until it breaks down or until Star Trek transporter technology could be made available and eliminate the need for cars and bridges altogether. Apparently, due to some mix up in customs with the Heisenberg subspace field compensator, the cracks came first.

The suspension of reality bridges are already here. We will proceed Monday morning to this and that side of the Sava without major interruption. We will continue to curse the bridges and traffic. We will continue to dream of easily flowing traffic from New to old Belgrade. We will suspend our disbelief that it will ever be done in our lifetimes. And we will suspend the belief that it will be our car which will be the last to cross the Gazela bridge before it crumbles.

You have the bridge, Scotty. Stand by to transport.

The Guns of Midnight

We can be pleased to know that Serbia's Top Cop thinks New Year's Eve 2009 went without a hitch. This does not mean that no accidents happened – we will find out about that soon enough – but "there were no injuries by firearms."

Fireworks? No, firearms.

The use of guns in holiday festivities, although it seems to be waning in the Serbian capital, is still a source of trepidation for most of us mild-mannereds and law abiders. I still remember stories of a poor soul who hid behind closed shutters in his New Belgrade apartment only to be shot and killed anyway by a stray bullet which was shot in the air under the bacchanal frenzy of welcoming the New Year. Or the story of the lady who, many blocks away from any action, was beaned by a descending bullet finding its way back to earth, and went less-than-gently into the good night. These stories may be Belgrade apocrypha, or just urban myth, but when you see guns pointed at the air from windows, it makes you wonder what could happen.

When I was a boy, in rural Iowa, we were all banned from touching fireworks. My father or my grandfather handled the bottle rockets, firecrackers, and roman candles. We were warned of the dangers of putting out eyes and blowing off fingers. But no one told me that people were actually taking up real weapons in a shootout against the New Year...

And yet, the Los Angeles Times ran an article last month where the police warned citizens that it was a felony to shoot guns at midnight, while the Miami Herald quoted a police major saying shooting guns was "ridiculous and stupid."

So it is not only here...

Shooting at midnight, although I have never indulged (much less ever handled a gun at all), must give a sense of power. It must feel wildly uncivilized and free. To be able to cause a huge noise from an instrument whose intended purpose is to kill or injure living beings must bring an unfettered sense of Man's Dominion over the World. It is a declaration of Imperium in Imperio.

That is until someone gets killed.

In the meantime, the main source of New Year's tragedy comes from road accidents. The deathtoll at holidays is always higher than usual and one town in the US state of Georgia brought a grim solution. A funeral parlor was offering free funerals to anyone who stated that they would be drinking and driving on New Year's Eve.

What does it all mean? Does it mean that we need danger and the threat of death to really enjoy ourselves? Do we need to appease the gods of the new year with ritual sacrifice? It seems we squeezed into 2010 without major incident, which should be good news. But perhaps the news only means that we are in for trouble this year.

No worry. We still have Serbian New Year ahead to tip the balance.

Happy New Year, everyone.

(Don't shoot anybody.)

Emasculating the Cowboys

Due to the new law on traffic, I am currently in the market for trading in my car for an elephant. Please contact this blog with photo and details. Camels also will be considered. No time wasters please.

Given that the cameras will apparently be rolling all the time, there will be no place for the White City's traffic cowboys to hide. By cowboy, I am referring to the guy in the black Audi, with no license numbers, slaloming from right to left to right lanes at 130 kph while talking on one cell phone, texting on another, lighting a cigarette, changing the CD music, and wearing dark glasses behind tinted windows.

At midnight.

Either these cowboys will be gelded and stabled by the all-seeing eyes in the sky, or they will become the single largest source of income for Belgrade traffic police.

We see these cowboys every day. We sit behind our wheels and curse them under our breath. We hope that they get caught and fined. But while we seethe and watch them, we know that the likely recipients of the tickets will be us. We are the low hanging fruit, easy wins for the cops.

As much as I am very much in favor of reigning in the terror of the streets, I am also a little afraid of these new techno-informants. No matter what you do, you cannot always get everything right in the car. You forget the seat belt (well, I do anyway), you speed up to 42 in a 40 zone, you cruise through a yellow light that turns red before you make it all the way.

Petty infractions, to be sure, but with the cameras snapping, you have no one to whom to make your case. The incriminating photos arrive at your home accompanied by your ticket. In the old days (i.e., last week), you could cajole and banter a little with the traffic cop and head off a ticket on the grounds of reasonableness or a small consideration. But to argue a camera ticket, you will have to go before a judge – and who will do that?

So, my guess is that the best way to deal with this Brave New World is to step into an older one. I do not believe the new laws apply to elephants. I will have no trouble with parking as he can rove around the park while he waits for me. I will have no trouble with speeding because the elephant could never work up enough velocity.

Seat belts may be tricky, however.

Pandemic Pandemonium

Whenever things start going horribly wrong, someone always tells us not to panic. As soon as they tell us not to panic, we sagely nod our heads and then, collectively, start to freak out.

The official name for the flu which is putting so many into hospitals and claiming lives around the world (and here in Serbia) is the "pandemic H1N1/09 virus." They have to call it by its long name because "H1N1" is just the regular flu.

Pandemics should have fancy names, names which inspire fear and loathing. Marketeers behind the "The Black Plague" had it right. There is nothing scarier than that. H1N1 sounds like a form to fill in when doing your taxes.

"Did you carry over any deductions?"

"Yes, here's my H1N1."

But names aside, panic is beginning to balloon into pandemic proportions. Many people have taken to wearing surgical masks around in the streets. A great many others have decided to avoid the streets altogether. Home remedies are pulled out of the closets – onions, honey, beets, and sour cabbage juice. Some people are saying it is passed around by coughing and sneezing; some say it is all about skin contact. I saw several people in the supermarket yesterday wearing gloves.

But maybe they were just cold.

In the end, we do not really know enough about this virus to know what to do about it yet. The best advice, if you ask me, is to AVOID PEOPLE. This way, if you have the virus you do not spread it, and if you do not have it, you might not get it. On the other hand, it could be airborne as well – so AVOID PEOPLE and AVOID BREATHING.

According to one website, there are five things you can do:

Get enough vitamin D (since we get a lot of it from the sun, the winter will not help)

Try not to touch things and people and wash your hands (this goes with my AVOID PEOPLE idea).

Rinse nose and throat regularly (Ok… what to say about that?)

Get enough sleep (Difficult if you are up nights worrying about being infected)

Eat garlic (This way people will avoid YOU)

This is probably all good common-sense advice. It is probably all right, and it could be all wrong. The problem we have in knowing what to do and how to behave is that there are too many different ideas about. We panic because we do not have clear and irrefutable instructions that will help us avoid catching the pandemic virus.

In light of this, I am revising my advice: AVOID ADVICE.

Especially mine.

Park Place

In the White City on the Danube, there are at least a ZILLION cars. I have counted them. Unfortunately for us, denizens of the city, there are only about 27 parking places. Three are reserved for handicapped drivers. 23 are reserved for government.

From 06.00 to 24.00.

Naturally this introduces an element of competition into the free-for-all that is loosely called "parking" in any major European capital. At any given point during the day, half of the city is trawling for a coveted parking spot. They drive slowly down the side streets. Their eyes are narrowed and darting left and right. If you are close enough, you can see the muscles of their jaws set a little tighter than usual. Some of them are sweating feverishly.

In the meantime, the other half of the Belgrade driving population is stepping blithely from their driver's seats, locking their doors, and giving a smug in-your-face gloating grin to the slow-motion parade. "We found a place! Why can't you?"

"Nah, nah, nah-nah, nah!"

Aggression nearly always spikes dramatically in people when they are driving under any circumstances. We scream obscenities, gesticulate, and turn, forcibly smiling, to our children in the back seat and say: "I am just showing you how NOT to behave." In the meantime, some guy has nicked your rear-view mirror while your head was turned. More yelling.

It takes relatively little to spark an explosion in a typical driver. Anyone who hesitates more than half a second in traffic is demonized. Anyone who switches lanes in front of us, who signals left and turns right, who stops abruptly, who is trying to talk on the phone while driving, or who checks out something in their teeth in the mirror is suddenly a blood enemy.

But when it comes to parking, our tempers rise astronomically from the already heightened circumstances of normal driving. I have seen people leap from their vehicles, ready to engage in actual fisticuffs to defend their right to a parking place. Of course, once people step out of their cars, their epinephrine levels return to more normal levels, and people need to make an effort to overcome the instinct not to punch the other guy's lights out.

We tolerate precious little from people who park. They always take too long, try too many times to get it right, spend an eternity trying to fit a jeep into a "Fića" sized spot (before they finally give up and hold up traffic a few meters further along the street). Among the moves which score highest in Aggressively Provocation are the zippy drivers who sneak in and steal a place for which you have been 'patiently' waiting. These guys pretend they do not see you, slip into the spot in one quick movement, suddenly become deaf to your blaring horn-honking protests, and then will coyly turn to you and give a moderately concerned look which says "Is something wrong?" In response, your arms fly out their sockets as you wave them wildly to indicate that it was YOUR space and that you had been waiting half an hour (it's always half an hour, even if it was only three minutes). In general they will shrug and walk away quickly, leaving you spot-less.

The other one that never fails to enrage is the micro-mini car trying to parallel park in a space large enough for an articulated lorry. Here the frustration builds because you just KNOW that you could have parked in that same place an hour before the micro car started making its moves. You wait as they approach, look out the window, back up a little, approach again, look again, back up again – each changing of gears ratchets up the rage another painful notch. I have come very close to leaving my car and offering to park it for them, rather than watch the excruciating scene any longer.

Maybe I should just buy a bus pass.

Bear-Stapling in Belgrade

Having taken my son to the zoo recently, it occurs to me that I might spend a few choice words and criticism of the appalling conditions (my opinion) suffered by the animals interned in the Belgrade Zoo. I might, since it is my chosen form and inexorable proclivity, choose to use irony to express my feelings. Instead of saying

The Belgrade Zoo has animal enclosures which are not big enough, I might rather say:

In the case of the polar bear, for example, the Belgrade zookeepers might save further space by merely encasing the great bear in cling-film and affixing him to the wall with large staples.

In the first instance, the statement is TRUE but BANAL. In the second case, you as readers are allowed to feel the pain of the polar bear, already living in cramped conditions. But which is actually a more effective way to make the point?

It seems to be the case that True and Banal works better. This is because the concept of irony, when applied by a foreigner in Serbia (my status), is too often interpreted quite literally. If I published sentence B about the cling-film, then I would be hunted down for everything from cruelty to animals, incitement to revolution within the zoological community, wholesale denigration of the Serbian state, to wrongful employment of Large Staples.

Strange as it might seem, however, I do not think for a moment that bear-stapling is to be advocated or encouraged in any way.

Irony is used as an indirect way to draw attention to existing conditions and maybe make people aware of them who either do not know or have not formed an opinion about them. The hope is that people will read solution B and say to themselves, "are the animals really so compactly confined?" And what do I hope to achieve by eliciting that kind of thought? Only a return to statement A ("Belgrade zoo has animal enclosures which are not big enough"), armed with a stronger emotional response.

Although I am sure I will come back to the subject of the zoo in another entry, I would like to concentrate on the use of irony. Irony, satire, parody, and sarcasm: these are the stock in trade of anyone writing from am Anglo-Saxon viewpoint. These are also linguistic-cultural barriers. We use these forms to write about very important issues, but without the high seriousness and self-absorption of the politician, the theologian, the university professor, or the animal rights activist. It does not mean, however, that the issues are any less important. It is used to alert people to reality by using farce and fantasy.

Jonathon Swift, in his well-known essay "A Modest Proposal," says that the Irish should eat their babies in order to avoid the suffering of living in poverty. This is neither a serious call to cannibalism nor an Irish joke: this is Swift's sharp-edged way of pointing out the severity of poverty in Ireland at the time when he was writing. If he had chosen to write: "The Irish are very poor and hungry," who would have understood the depth of desperation facing that people?

Every culture has Panic Buttons that writers should only touch if they are willing to accept an avalanche of criticism by people who are easily offended and take themselves extremely seriously. In the US, they include everything from Washington's war policy to school prayer to bilingual education. In Serbia, it seems that the list is longer, and any statement that is remotely perceived as less than complimentary to Serbia is construed to be a brutal attack on the nation and its people. And while we all know that the world is not short of wackos and crackpots who actually advocate extremism, we also know that the problems exist and will not magically disappear because we do not dare to talk about them.

Poverty is a scourge on a global scale; mistreatment of exotic animals in zoos (not only Belgrade by far) is an easily avoided tragedy. They are not equal, to be sure, but they are real. By telling you this, you should (and please do) tell me to propose solutions and not just complain. But the solutions that both Swift and I propose (and I beg you to forgive the circumstantial self-aggrandizement of lumping myself into the same league as Swift) may be SO extreme as to suggest a more reasonable approach.

Now, while you are thinking about that, I have a few more bears to staple.

Welcome to Here!

There is abundant evidence to support the hypothesis that I am writing to you now from Serbia. Although I do not feel under any obligation to prove to you where I am, I certainly do not feel the need for someone to tell ME where I am.

And then along comes the Tourist Organization of Serbia.

All around Belgrade this summer, billboards and posters have sprung up. They have pictures of enticing foods, they have catchy slogans luring the idle passer-by to dream about voyages to exotic places. When you look closer, you see that (Hey!) it is the food you had for lunch, and (Wait!) this is advertising for Serbia!

Hang on… aren't we already here?

Indeed we are, we in Belgrade respond. Why then, we ask ourselves, has the TOS decided to spend a lot of money for an advertising campaign promoting Serbia to Serbs and the rest of us here? This is where we began: I am sure I do not need them to tell me where I am.

When we travel to a foreign country (let's say Burkina Faso for example), we usually do so by a conscious act of free will. Therefore when we land in Ouagadougou, we do not need to be convinced to come to Burkina Faso. We have already bought that concept. Maybe a nice poster showing us the Park of Bangr Weogo or the sacred crocodiles of Sabou would be better…

A campaign for Serbia would be good, say, in another country where potential holidaymakers are at sixes and sevens about where to holiday-make. They might see a poster of delicious kajmak and sarma and say, "Ok honey, let's go to Serbia." However, the posters are written in Cyrillic characters, and the local holidaymaker from, say, Sheffield would have a hard time making it out. She might say, "Ok honey, let's go to Russia."

I begin to wonder about the target audience of this campaign. It is not foreign tourists, as anyone seeing them has already chosen to come here. It is not Western European tourists, because we cannot read the symbols. Who is it for anyway?

One possibility is that it is aimed at all of us, encouraging us to stay home for the holidays. Another possibility is that it is for accidental tourists who boarded a train in Istanbul thinking they were headed for Plovdiv but overslept and ended up in Belgrade. In this case, they might spring out of the compartment, stretch their legs and see these posters. "Serbia," they would say. "That sounds good! Let's go there!"

"But you are already here," the conductor would say.

"Splendid!"

Admittedly, this scenario does not seem entirely likely, but stranger things can happen. After all, there has to be a reason for creating such a lovely campaign for Serbia (and it is very nicely done) and placing it right here at home.

Can anyone help me understand this?

CONSUMERS & OTHER ANIMALS

CONSUMERS & OTHER ANIMALS

We want nothing more than to serve you! If you want it, we got it!
We have it in blue, in green, and in stripes.
We have your size in the back.
We take special orders.

But you can't have it. I'm busy.

When something gets your goat and gets your dander up at the
same time, you know that the situation will soon be escalating.
For me, the best way to make this happen is to send me shopping in Belgrade. By now, when shopkeepers see me coming,
they run.

Five Words

When an older friend of mine, having seen and instantly fancied a brand new mobile phone in a Belgrade shop window, she had no idea the ordeal that was about to begin.

She entered and began browsing the other phones (one should always do a little comparative shopping), to which the shop-keeper – a young girl more occupied with her own mobile and nails than her customers – indelicately shouted out, "MAY I HELP YOU?"

A little put off by the attitude, my friend nevertheless began to ask questions. She wanted to know the price. She wanted to know about the package deals with telecom providers. Then she wanted to know about how the phone worked. And could she hold it? Is it better than other similar models? Can I go onto the Internet? How does that work? The shopkeeper's patience, how-ever, came to an abrupt halt after the first question.

"We are not a SCHOOL," she grumbled.

And thus we enter into the great consumer conundrum of Ser-bian shopping. If you want to buy something, you should have already informed yourself quite deeply on it. You should have studied the question in the privacy of your own home. You should have consulted other people in the areas which both-ered you. You should, moreover, eliminate all other choices you might have in order to cut down on time spent browsing in the shop. In other words, you must know EXACTLY what you want and EVERYTHING about it. This way you can obtain the object at the expense of one gesture and an exchange of five words:

"That," pointing. "Cash or card?" "Card"

"Pin?"

The hellos, goodbyes, and thank yous are all (of course) op-tional and generally unnecessary. After all, we will not become friends with this shopkeeper and invite her over for our slavas.

My friend, sadly, did not know all of these prerequisites and, being talkative and inquisitive by nature, asked her questions and tried to engage the unaccommodating girl in incommodious conversation. When the girl closed the "school," my friend told her she would NOT buy it from her and walked out indignantly.

What did the girl learn from this? She lost nothing by not selling a phone. She missed an SMS on her own phone. And I think she might have broken a nail. Three more customers like this and she would have to take a day off to relieve the stress.

The Customer is always right? Not in MY shop!

Shopping Ourselves to Recovery

The best thing we can do, in this time of economic crises, is to go shopping.

There has long been an unwritten psychological boon which comes with this. We shop when we are feeling down. We shop when we are feeling good. We feel empowered even if we do not buy anything. The very idea that we COULD decide to exchange money for the goods on display before us is a powerful notion.

Our new shopping complex at Ušće is another example of this. Never mind that we are teetering on the edge of solvency. Never mind that the new Ušće mall is a rearranged replica of Delta City. Who cares about uncertain finances, unemployment, inflation, and rising taxes? We can just buy a new pair of pants and all will pass.

I sound cynical, I know. But in reality I do believe in consumerism. The consumer is the one piece on the chess board that can move anywhere it wants. It can leap from one side of the board to the other even more ably than the queen. When the consumer's voice is heard, the rest of society redeploys itself to accommodate it.

Why?

Western capitalism. It is predicated on the consumer. We produce commodities and merchandise in large quantities to trade for money. With the money, we build more and we buy more. We have service providers who tell us what to do with our money, what to buy, what to do with what we bought, and how to tell everyone around us how cool we are.

The consumer's place as a link in the chain is immutable, and when the consumer decides to stay home, the whole economy trembles.

Therefore let us have another fifteen shopping malls in Belgrade! We need to draw the consumer out of his hiding place and into the aisles. As a side note, perhaps it is also a good thing that we do not have a lot of choice in shops. Maybe the monopolists are helping us become better consumers by hypnosis. We see the same shops over and over again until finally we feel they are part of our mental landscape.

If we had real consumer choices, not those dictated by one or two people from their yachts, we might become confused. We might wander aimlessly without BUYING anything. An embarrassment of choice is a burden on the much needed Shopping Automaton. We are, or so it seems to be, incapable of making informed choices in shopping. We need easy, binary choices.

Zeros or ones.

So far, the zeros seem to have it.

Tales of Retail Retold

So there I was at Cartier, Rue de la Paix 11, in Paris. I asked the guy to show me what he had in watches for around four million euros. He assessed me with a glance (jeans, Indian kurta shirt, sneakers) and he said, "We have none. I am going to go eat my lunch."

They were Nike sneakers by the way. Originals.

His judgment was that I was not of a sufficient seriousness or stature to look at his precious merchandise. Generally speaking, when someone comes into a shop and wants to see something in a specific price range, he's a BUYER. If he were a Browser (O! Hated Species!), he would probably just shuffle around the gold-threaded carpeting and head off quickly. But here, I was cast off because I was not worthy of his time.

Naturally this was a cause of annoyance for me.

However, it was not REALLY Cartier in Paris. Nor was it a watch I was looking for. In fact I was in the White City on the Danube, at Zeleni Pijac, trying to buy a watch *band* (price: RSD 200). I came over to the stand and was looking through the watch bands. The lady behind the table said, "What-do-you-want," as usual, although the tone rather seemed to tell me to go to hell. And I said: *I want pizza, can't you see? That's why I am looking at your watch bands!*

But then *out loud* I said… that I needed a watch-band for this watch (removes watch and shows her). She takes it, looks at it, examines it, and then says: I don't work here, ask my husband. Privately, I am getting a bad feeling about all this. She called to the husband who was very busily occupied in a nasal excavation project in the adjacent stall.

GUY: What?

ME: Do you have a band this size?

He digs for a second. I dig with him. I showed him one I liked, and he threw down four in a huff and said, "NEMA. And I am going to eat my lunch."

I am still not certain as to what offense I gave, but he stormed away as if my intention to plunk down only 200 dinars was not worthy of his time. I wondered what he could possibly expect from me. He only sells watch bands. Should I have asked to buy 1,000 bands?

Once again, I was left disgruntled by retail. My crazy theory about retail is that if you are selling, your main goal is to sell. But it seems that I am wrong. The main goal of many shopkeepers and retailers is to be left alone. A customer, like me for example, should come in to a shop and excuse himself for disturbing the people there. He should know precisely what he wants beforehand. No browsing. No "just looking."

Most of the time, if you do know what you want, you REALLY have to want it badly because the first response is always "nema." Then you have to explain how you need it a lot and that it looks a little like this and has these functions. Then they will sigh heavily, drop their shoulders, and condescend to reach over to their left and get the thing you want.

This is the retail power play. They need to establish dominion of the customer so he feels obliged to take something – maybe not even what he wants – just to cover the offense of daring to walk into the shop. If the shopkeeper starts pandering to the whims of customers, it will never end! Sure, he will probably sell more and get repeat business. But he will lose the upper hand.

In fairness, of course every place is not like this. In some they will ignore you. In some they will stay on the phone until you get tired and leave. In Paris (not rue de la Paix but rue de Sèvres), I remember standing in line at a bakery, a line that stretched all the way out into the street, while the two behind the counter were just chit-chatting together. After five minutes or so, one turned to us and said: next?

I have decided on a five-point strategy that seems to allow me to get through my longish shopping list.

1. DON'T ASK! If you don't see it, it is not there.

2. If you have to ask, make it negative: "You probably don't have any toothbrushes, do you?"

3. Gather as much stuff as you can in your basket BEFORE asking anything, so they see you are serious.

4. Dress up for shopping.

5. Make friends with the shopkeeper – sympathize about the heat, inflation, the trees on Bulevar, the highway works in progress… Then spring your question. Maybe show pictures of your kids.

This will not work every time, Dear Readers, and it requires a lot of practice as well as reversing Normal Attitudes to shopping, but it can help.

Now I am just off to the kiosk to beg and cajole the guy for a newspaper.

Sell-By Dating

Unlike a good Bordeaux wine, yoghurt, cheese, milk, meat, and mayonnaise do not acquire greater palatability with age.

Yet there are still shops and supermarkets which do not seem to have grasped this distinction, placing the recent produce and goods at the back of the shelves while proudly displaying food-stuffs long since passed their expiration dates to the fore.

Although it is true that, no matter where we are, consumers should *always* read the packaging and the sell-by dates before investing in comestibles, it is also true that I never really paid close attention to them before coming to live here. In fact, my surmise (wrong- headed though it was) was always to assume that the grocer had my Best Interests at heart. That no one would EVER make an attempt on my life by trying to flog off 30-year old tinned meat on an unwitting consumer public.

Nor, by the way, would I even think about buying tinned meat, but that is a story for another time...

And yet, one fine day while going through the cupboard at home so as to compose a shopping list, I discovered that nearly everything I had bought the previous week had expiry dates that looked more like the ages of my children than shelf-life indicators. Clearly I should have looked more carefully in buying it, but – I ask you – ALL of it was from days gone by?

This incident happened a few years ago, and since I have been more vigilant, but now there new factors which perplex and befuddle the ingenuous consumer. The science of marking packages with expiration dates has become a game of smoke and mirrors. The date-stamp on the box or tin is no longer enough.

Consider the concepts of the "packing" date, the "sell-by" date, and the "purchase by" date. At times (often with eggs), they will only tell you when they stuck the eggs in the box. Does this actually indicate the age of the eggs? And if you are given a "sell by" date, who is being protected here? The consumer is generally not selling the food forward. Perhaps it should read: Sell by this date to avoid prosecution.

The "purchase by" date is another conundrum. Once you have purchased it (presumably before the indicated time), how many minutes do you have to consume it before it turns into toxic waste?

All of this has then to be balanced against the frightening thought of sell-by dates which are marked as being in the distant future. I have seen packaged mortadella which will allegedly remain edible for eight months after buying it. The greyish colour of the meat to one side, the expiration date is right – so it MUST be ok, we think.

In the meantime, I have employed a team of paleontologists to come shopping with me next week.

Parts and Labor Pains

Having now invested a significant amount of cash into the Delta Money Pit (this is the technical term for the garage where my perfectly operating car has been transformed into a terminal patient), I am now investing my time.

Yesterday, as a kind of joke, I was informed that my car was "ready" to pick up. Two weeks ago I had stupidly brought it here to have a check-up – oil, filters, and yada, yada, yada. I should have immediately seen the sodomy in their eyes when they said I had to leave the car for two days even to get an estimate.

It turns out that my motor was slightly dirty and therefore would have to be replaced – naturally no one at the DMP would ever *dream* of fixing a part that could be ordered from far off Italy, shipped by a horse cart, and used to extort the equivalent of the Argentine national debt from me.

The best part of all this is what comes now: I said, "Ok!"

For them, this might have been an even better response than merely dropping my trousers and bending over. As it happens, I had consented to this for the whole company, in perpetuity, whenever the spirit moves them.

14 days and thousands of euros later, I sit outside the garage watching the Experts attempting to turn off my rear passenger lights. I am now into the fourth hour of my vigil. It appears that while they were replacing every moving part of my poor car, one of the mechanics was hungry and began chewing on some exposed electrical cable.

At this stage, I can no longer leave. I am utterly committed to watching on as they tear the guts out of my car in the bootless search for the custom-made sabotage of the under-fed mechanic. I have passed blithely from anger to rage, from rage to righteous fury, from righteous fury to melancholy, and from melancholy to cynicism, and I am currently cultivating Rye and

Amused Detachment. This last, if I can sustain it, is probably best for my cardiac longevity.

(And since my heart is no longer under guarantee, I should be wary of someone here ordering a replacement...)

And now here I sit, on location, with plenty of time to write this blog on my phone. I mention as a by-the-way that, while writing this, I managed to drop the phone and crack the display (another Customer Service blog may be expected soon when they will want to mail my phone to Helsinki to fix it).

Hour Five is beginning now. I came to the doctor for a runny nose, was given brain surgery, and found that they broke my toe during the operation. In watching them trying to find the problem for five hours, my trust in the rest of the million-dollar job has been somewhat destabilized.

Dear Reader, I am low on batteries, patience, and cigarettes by now. The Alfa Romeo now lies prone and dismembered on the garage floor. And I have no idea how and in what way Humpty-Dumpty will be reanimated.

I close this chapter inconclusively and hope that when archeologists find my remains here that they might unravel this mystery to a more satisfying end.

And that the rear lights will have been turned off.

Loan Gunman

Let's begin by stating the Obvious.

A banker's first and best duty is, of course, to extract all the money from your pocket, mattress, closet, or left shoe and lock it up securely in its vaults.

Never mind all of the advertising you have seen to the contrary telling us about FREE CASH, NO INTEREST, SWISS FRANCS, and Gosh-my-bank-wants-to-buy-me-a-new-house! In the end, your dinars must wind up on the other side of the teller's counter, ostensibly waiting for you to collect them later, otherwise we would have a lot fewer bankers clogging the arteries of Belgrade with Mercedes, BMWs, and Jaguars.

(If I were a banker, I think I would be the guy in the Aston Martin.)

Given this goal, is it any surprise that, when you walk into any of the hundreds of branches of our 36 banks, the first one to greet you with a smile and cold steel is the armed security guard?

Immediately they want to know what you are doing there. Immediately, you want to put your hands in the air and beg for a deposit form (don't ask for the *withdrawal* form or he might think you were asking for a quick-draw, leading to a sub-optimum banking experience…).

As a receptionist, the gunslinger is quite effective, if not the perfect picture of *politesse*. Once he has determined that you have legitimate business in the bank, he scans the room and sends you to the longest possible line. The teller on the far left – the one that says "All Transactions" – is normally empty. As you stand in the serpentine double-file that seems to snake around the entire exposed surface area of the bank's atrium, your eyes dart constantly to the teller who is busy filing her nails.

Questions come to mind….

What would happen if the Bank Sniper thought your business was not good enough to afford you access to the bank? Does he shoot you then?

If so, who is responsible for the bodies?

What is that teller over there doing?

Why is this line double-file?

Can I get shot for changing lines?

What time is it already?

The mind boggles with such imponderables at moments like this. It is only then that you realize that all of this has happened in about four minutes. This is another intriguing mystery of the banking world: the improbable elongation of physical time. You look around yourself and check out the other banking clients… One brought a pillow and blanket; one brought a book; one has been talking to someone called "Brate" for about seven hours on his mobile phone (within, of course, the confines of the four minutes you have been there… don't ask).

Then there's the guy ahead of you. You came to the bank to do ONE THING. This is another way of announcing to the rest of the bank patrons: "I am stupid." The guy ahead of you has about fifteen dog-eared bank books, three forms of identity, a stack of papers with stamps and signatures, a Samsonite overnight case bulging with files and folders. In short, the guy ahead of you has WAITED ALL HIS LIFE to come to the bank and he will transact 53 years worth of business in front of the teller, while you stand there getting varicose veins, grey hair, closer to your pension (for which you will need a different form and may have to go to the back of the line again), and try to remember what that ONE THING you wanted to do in the bank was after all….

In the meantime, the Loan Gunman has his eye trained on you. If you become distracted, engrossed in contemplating the mismatched socks of the guy ahead of you (one was *really* dark blue – it could happen to anyone, I suppose), the marksman may identify you as a target and whisper to the lady behind you to step ahead of you in line. Want to complain?

"Draw," he challenges.

K.F.C.C.C.P.

My grandmother and her cousin Lula were always in competition with the Colonel.

When I was a boy in the Iowa cornfields (actually we lived in a house), the making of fried chicken happened with blissful regularity. My sister and I would be whisked from kitchen to kitchen to consume fried chicken. I have a distinct recollection of telling Lula that her chicken tasted *better* than the Colonel's.

Immortality achieved.

With this as a background, I must admit that since those bucolic days of yesteryear until only very recently, I had not paid a single visit on Colonel Sanders (*now a license rather than a name*) or Kentucky Fried Chicken (*as we once knew it, now a mere abbreviation,* KFC). During these more than 30 intervening years, this purveyor of extra crispy and coleslaw was off my Fast Food Radar (which, by the way makes, the Hubble Space Telescope look like a Kinder egg sneak-a-scope).

And then the Colonel came to Serbia.

Unfortunately, back in Kentucky, the good old marketing boys at KFC had neglected to read newspapers during these 30 years. No one told them, for example, that cold war had ended, that the Soviet Union had fallen, that communists were not the biggest global annoyance any more. I suppose it did not seem to matter with your feet in the blue grass.

But then someone had the Bright Idea to send KFC abroad. By the time they had come to the S's on the list, seen *Serbia*, called in an expert geographer to show them where it was on the map, figured out that it used to hide inside of *Yugoslavia* (in the Y's much further down), the world had changed again many times over.

The good old marketing boys, however, had been busy. They invented KFCommunism. They reckoned it would be useful for all them there commie-countries over there east of England (i.e., everything else until Japan).

Before you start calling this in as a hoax, dear readers, I invite you to visit KFC here in New Belgrade…. Lights, please?

(*Fade in – KFC counter – Delta City*)

- Can I help you?

- I would like a Picnic bucket

- Ok

- With only dark meat please

(*cue Scary Music – maybe from Scooby Doo*)

- Only dark?

- Yes please.

- You can't have that.

- Why not?

- I don't know… Let me get the manager.

(*Exits left, running*)

(*Enter* **Manager** *left – cue Imperial March from Star Wars*)

- What seems to be the problem? (heavy breathing through black strap-on asthma inhaler)

- I ordered a Picnic bucket with all dark meat.

- No.

(Pause)

- No?

- No you cannot have that.

- But I ordered it. You have the chicken don't you?

- Yes (breathing), we do.

(Pause)

- Then can I order only pieces?

– Yes.

– Good. Then I will have three drumsticks and three thighs please.

– No.

Several hours later, a young man looking nervously at me called me aside and explained what was going on. I could NOT buy which ever pieces I wanted because there were not enough of them. But, I pointed out, I can SEE THEM SITTING THERE! Yes, he told me, there are enough in an Absolute Sense. But there are *not enough to go around*.

Light dawned.

Under capitalism, I could order every last piece of chicken, every cole of slaw, and the manager's pointy hat if I wanted (maybe even the inhaler to boot). And they would sell it to me. But under KFCommunism, I must think about the Collective. What would happen if, say, three hours later a young couple came looking for a Picnic bucket and found ONLY WHITE meat? Imagine their shock and despair! No, as a consumer under this regime, it is more important to think for the society before yourself. My allotment of dark meat is two (maybe three if you play golf with the party boss) .

I should NOT be so selfish. I should NOT think only of what I want... Do you want this to turn into the bedlam of a Consumer Society?? Certainly not! Back in Kentucky, the good old marketing boys had thought of this. They were probably strumming the banjo in glee right now to see how well their KFCommunism worked.

In the meantime, I consulted my watch, noticed that it was the 21st century, and came up with my own cunning plan:

(*Enter* **Me**, *again, stage right*)

– May I have one chicken leg, to take away, please?

– Yes.

– Thank you.

(*Pays, exits right*)

(Pause)

(*Enter* **Me**, *again, stage right*)

– May I have one chicken leg, to take away, please?

– Yes.

– Thank you.

(*Pays, exits right*)

(Pause)

(*Enter* **Me**, *again, stage right*)

– May I have one chicken leg, to take away, please?

– Yes.

– Thank you.

(*Pays, exits right*)

I did this ten times, got what I wanted in the end, and headed home. When I got back to my flat, with the chicken now on a descending scale of coldness, I immediately called three or four major American dailies and subscribed the Colonel and his minions to each.

It is time for the fall of the KFCCCP. The Cold Chicken War is gone.

No Change

Burek, bread, yoghurt, and that was it. A thousand dinar note. It was all I had.

From behind the (apparently empty) cash register, she looked at me in utter disgust. She said: "No," and moved on the next guy without waiting for me to vacate the spot. I had forfeited my right to buy *anything* – if I understood this exchange at all – because she could not make change for 1,000 dinars.

I am beginning to think that having a low tolerance for poor customer service is actually doing me a huge disservice while I live here. My instinct was to be outraged, but instead I counted to ten.

I waited for Mr. I-Have-the-Right-Change-ha-ha behind me to receive HIS burek (mine actually) and his bright smile (clearly, NOT mine), then I tried again. By this time, however, and I did not realize it yet, I had become invisible. She looked directly through my expectant pleading face to see the Bag Lady behind me, and the Newspaper-Reading Guy behind her.

Out I walked.

But there was no option of returning home without the bag full of grease-laden starches. So I needed a new plan. Next door, there was a small toy shop. I went inside, hoping to buy my son a little something and break the massive 1000 dinar note. I was immediately attacked by the previously sleeping sales person who leapt to his feet and shouted IZVOLITE! at me. About five centimeters from my nose.

I said I was just looking, and he backed off a little. I wanted to find a toy that would 1) allow me to be a hero when I brought it home, and 2) would get me the magical change to buy the burek. The sales person stationed himself exactly between me and the plastic Chinese toys. Each time I reached toward the shelf, he mirrored me. When finally his defensive actions made me start to feel like the criminal he clearly took me for, I discovered the solution. A Spiderman action figure: 502 dinars. My single stone was about to whack two birds!

Again the 1000 dinar note was produced. He took it handily and returned me a crisp 500 dinar note. NO! I protested! I did not have the two dinars change – he would HAVE to give me 498 dinars back! Little did he know I would have been willing to settle for 200 dinars if only to be able to get the bread which was still held firmly behind the disdainful eyes of the baker next door.

"Get me next time," he said affably. No change.

With low expectations, I went back to the bakery, asked again for the burek, bread, and yoghurt, and presented the 500 in trepidation. She sighed heavily, and turned to fill my order. Although I kept a poker face, I was jubilant inside! But then she turned back to me.

"No more burek," she droned. "Sold out."

Heads or Tails

SLAVONSKI BROD, CROATIA. Life makes for bad reading. Our daily stories do not have connecting plot lines, suspense and denouements, consequential trains of thought. Aristotle said stories should have beginnings, middles, and ends.

But life has only the middle.

Thus it is with this little Saga of Slavonia. Things just keep happening. With each flip of the coin, heads counter tails, tails best heads. And even though I am still in the middle of it, a certain heads-or-tails pattern emerges....

Heads: I made it to Zagreb yesterday in excellent time, early for my meeting

Tails: I got lost inside Zagreb for an hour and was late for my meeting.

Heads: I parked badly and asked meter guy how I should pay. He said don't worry (seeing I was a foreigner) that he would mark me paid and he walked 100 meters out of his way to show me where I should go for my meeting.

Tails: When I returned to the car there was a fat parking ticket.

Heads: After an excellent and useful meeting, I took again to the road, in good time to get home at a decent hour.

Tails: About an hour or so out of Zagreb, in Slavonski Brod, my car superheated and told me to stop.

Heads: The tow truck got to me within about 5 minutes.

Tails: It was the beginning of a 36-plus hour wait (in the middle of which I sit still).

Tails: no way to fix it tonight

Tails: MAYBE by tomorrow

Heads: They brought me to a little hotel (I am sure this was organized and happened many times before) where I should wait.

The hotel was nice, clean, and not a bad place to wait.

Tails: I had no other choice in the matter anyway.

Tails: I had not brought my chargers for computer or phone and my batteries were dying

Heads: Some other guest forgot his Nokia charger and I could use it.

If you try to tie all this together and make a Story out of it, you will come up short. The elements are all here for the plotline of a familiar movie. Out of town city guy gets stuck in the country side of another country, at the mercy of local gangster car mechanics and unable to return home.

By rights, if I wanted the story to end correctly, I should by now have made friends with all the local townspeople, organized a theatre event, saved a small child from being hit by a passing car, and be carried triumphantly on the shoulders of my new friends to my car which is working better than ever and for which the mechanic decides not to charge me!

Yeah, right…

Funny the things which can occur in the idle mind as it waits for the inevitable.

If I am still here by tomorrow at this time, be sure a new script will be ready for submission. Sadly my computer batteries will be long since dead and no one will hear my story.

Greetings and farewell from Slavonia!

Consumer Intimidation

Is the return of goods in Serbia a felony?

I am not sure that a proposal to criminalize the return of goods in a shop exists. In fact, I am not even sure that one does not ALREADY exist. Whatever the case, I now have a record. My JMBG number has been inscribed forever into the annals of whatever record-keeping authority monitors those nasty and dangerous consumers who wish to return something.

The Incident Report: Driving along on a Sunday under very hot temperatures and very slow highway conditions (as to be expected on both counts), my car began to complain that it was overheating. I pulled into a gas station and asked the guy to check the water. All ok. He was friendly enough to comply and help me out.

As it was a lazy Sunday, my hot and bothered Alfa Romeo with the hood up attracted a swarm of attendants at the gas station. Suddenly I felt like I was observing an experimental cardiac procedure in a teaching hospital. Each of the "doctors" leaned in and gave his opinion. As might be expected, the opinions outnumbered the attendants by a factor of two. But I stood by, grateful for the attention to the car, and let them run their differential diagnosis unimpeded.

At one stage, the conversation became as overheated as the car. One attendant, the Alfa Male as it were, raised his voice above all the others and declared: "ANTI-FREEZE!" The rest went quiet, and I followed the Alfa Male into the shop to obtain the prescription. Once back outside, however, the conclave had gathered strength. They rebelled against the diagnosis, and said there was no need for anti-freeze at all, just water.

Hm, ok, I hmmed. My confidence in this group was beginning to wane slightly. Still, I went back in with the guy to return the anti-freeze and swap it out for some distilled water. And this is where the incident occurred.

At the cash register, the girl told me I should see the manager and give some "details." I explained (obviously she did not know and I was feeling generous of spirit) that all she had to do was take back the anti-freeze, void the sale, and sell me the water. See the manager, she said.

The manager (I took his name subsequently) stood leaning on the end of the bar, about ten meters away from me. He eyed me suspiciously. He took out a notebook with forms. He wrote down the product name and then asked me for my identity card and JMBG. At this point, my Civil Rights Alarm started blaring in my ears.

Why in the name of God, I said in a mounting crescendo, should I EVER think about giving YOU my ID because your guy sold me the wrong thing? Take it back and sell me the other stuff. He insisted on the ID card and I flatly told him no. You do NOT need a record of me to take this back. I folded my arms indignantly. Why should you need it, I finally asked. And his reply was yet another spark of brilliance:

"Zakon."

So the law, I deduced, requires that a record be kept of returned goods and that the consumers who dare to return the goods are monitored. Our ID cards are transcribed into a ledger. We receive what is tantamount to a ticket. The whole process made me feel that I had somehow violated the law and would someday be held accountable for the un- purchased anti-freeze.

I have wracked my tired brain to try to find SOME excuse for this behavior, some reason which would show it is in my interest to be officially noted and ticketed for returning something. I cannot come up with anything. The manager, however, held his ground, and it became clear that he would not take anything back from me without my ID. I took HIS name and ID number (he was unfazed by this although he should have been as civically outraged as I).

Much has been made this year about protecting consumer rights. I suppose the first one is my right to remain silent – especially about anything I do not like or understand.

The Quick and the Stuck

Most guys like the old in-and-out.

When we go shopping, we tend to have a mental list of the four essential needs and want to get in and away from the shop as soon as humanly possible. Some of us will even time ourselves with the goal of bettering our time from the last attempt. This is what a good friend of mine calls "Ninja Shopping." The ninja shopper stays focused on the goal; he is not distracted by the promotions or the promoter-girls; he does not linger in indecision over a new kind of laundry powder.

Yet even the most practiced ninja shopper may be stymied by the notion of "convenience" in Serbia.

The other day, my friend, the Ninja Shopping Master, was sitting in front of me in a state of shock. His hand trembled over his coffee as he recounted for me his latest foray into the consumer experience. I listened carefully to his tale (also secretly gratified to know that these things do not happen ONLY to me) and took cautious heed.

The Master had entered the field of battle (Super Vero) equipped with the sure knowledge that he could engage, pick up his three items, and check out within six minutes, in time to meet me and gloat over his prowess.

Without slowing, he glided through the sliding doors, extending an arm and taking a red shopping basket, already aimed at the yoghurt section in the bank of refrigerated displays. Deftly avoiding the crowd milling about in fresh goods, he met his first obstacle in the biscuit aisle: the Jaffa Girl. With one strategic step, Jaffa Girl stopped his fluid motion and began to tell him about their biscuits. Undaunted, he smiled and thanked her and took her free sample – but a minute and a half had been lost.

Yogurt obtained, he scanned the path ahead. On the left, a stand with smoked ham; on the right, a suited figure from Alpha Bank; in the middle distance the soup aisle beckoned, and he cut through the straits directly toward it. He avoided both (although he heard them launch into their spiels as he passed), basketed the soup, and moved to last item – the toothpaste.

On the way to the toothpaste, he flanked toward frozen goods to approach the shelf unawares. In frozen goods, however, Pizza Girl awaited, alongside the Nespresso demonstrator. Unprepared, Scylla and Charybdis each robbed him of precious minutes as he sampled both coffee and pizza and took in their siren's banter.

The ticking clock however shook him free and he grabbed the last item and pushed through to the check out. Paid, bagged, ready, and at one step from freedom, he turned and found himself in utter defeat: Trolley Boy.

A row of empty trolleys blocked his egress, as Trolley Boy stood complacently chatting with Ivana from Check Out 3. The Master steamed. He cried out. He was fully stuck. Finally, in desperation, he shoved Trolley Boy with a shoulder and a look of unbridled rage. As Trolley Boy unhurriedly moved aside and the Master was free, he noted the time – 47 minutes.

Retail triumphs once again over the consumer.

Just for Show

Strolling through the walkways of one of our illustrious shopping malls last night, I was bludgeoned on the head.

The instrument used to whack me was a nicely crafted bit of Consumer Nonsense such as often seems to happen to me. The attack was unprovoked (or not very much so) and left me in a bit of a daze for hours after. Let me explain….

I was with friends who were shopping. This means that my role was to follow along and present the aspect of someone who was interested in the surrounding wares so as not to give the impression that was just idly following a shopper. It sounds much more complicated than it actually is. In an electronics emporium, I saw something that actually did catch my attention.

A television at which I could not look.

It was a new 3D television, made by a group of clever Japanese or Korean scientists in their secret laboratory. To look at it in its display, the average consumer gets a headache. The displacement of the red-green and red-blue spectrum kept making me want to look away from it. But the rest of the display was quite attractive, including the price which seemed very low for a TV which can produce a headache at will (usually it takes a good deal of channel surfing to develop one).

So, of course, I asked the salesman if I could look at it with the special 3D glasses. After all, if I am going to invest in this technology, I should need to inspect it and see if the effect is as compelling as it promises. There was a requisite sofa at the ready for such viewings, placed at about a two meters twenty from the screen. I extended my hand in anticipation of receiving the glasses and completing the experience.

He said no.

After a short moment, I wondered aloud how he expected anyone to buy this TV and why it was set up for a test viewing if the glasses could not be used. "We don't have any," said he. So, again wondering aloud, if I were to decide to buy this, it would be because I IMAGINE that I could have 3D TV at home. I would have to IMAGINE that I liked it better than the regular 2D to which I have been accustomed over my entire lifetime and give it all up on the POSSIBILITY that I would like this better?

No batteries.

No batteries? In the glasses you do not have? This was the moment when my head began to spin and the full brunt of the Consumer Nonsense came cracking down over my skull. I looked back at the TV and found that the blues and reds seemed to have separated even further. Someone had sat down on the viewing sofa and was watching, without glasses. I looked at him closely to see if he did not have 3D ocular implants or contact lenses.

The salesman, trained professional that he was, looked at me in silence. His mouth seemed to be slightly open. His eyes were challenging. They could have been saying one of two things: A) I cannot be bothered to go to the back and get the glasses for you because you are not really going to buy this tonight; or B) I don't know what the glasses look like – I used to sell shoes. I asked him how many of these 3D TVs he had sold.

None. This is just a display.

WARNING: In order to avoid this experience, we strongly suggest that you form a negative opinion of 3D television before shopping. This will abnegate the dilatory effects of circular logic and will be much easier on the salesman.

Join the Queue

The queue forms HERE.

Before the holidays, we were out in droves, standing in endless queues in shops, banks, boutiques, post offices, and supermarkets in order to get ready for the festivities. Now time has come to face the endless queues in shops, banks, boutiques, post offices, and supermarkets again. But this time it is for everyday life.

There is a very specific psychology to the consumer queue. At Christmas and New Year's, we suffer through them because we have to, because everyone else is doing it too, and because we did not have the foresight to prepare ourselves a week or so in advance. We run out to the supermarkets and shops to make last minute purchases, settle for what is left on the shelves because of the rush, and content ourselves to wait. And wait. And wait until it is finally our go at the till – only to find out that the credit card reader is on the fritz.

In "normal" times, however, such as the long stretch between now and the next Major Shopping Holiday into which we are now entering, the same queues are there but our tolerance for them is dramatically diminished. Now we grumble, shuffle our feet, and give meaningful looks to the people in front of us in the queue, careful not to look at the ones behind us as they apply the same treatment to our backs.

Queue stagnation has a number of root causes, each being more annoying than the next. The first is sheer human volume – too many people trying to do too much of the same thing at the same time. The rest of the causes are collateral damage from the first. There's Pay By Check Guy, who has to produce seventeen cards and proofs of identity, painstakingly fill up the check, give it a once over for errors, make the corrections, and then hand it to the cashier, who proceeds to verify all his verifications. Then there is Absent Minded Guy, who is unable to unload the basket, pay, pack the bags, and move along without long pauses and hesitations. Smartphone Guy is next – he slows down the queue by updating his Facebook status, sending emails, talking to two people at once, and sending text messages instead of playing his part in the queue.

The most conspicuously heinous of these villains, however, is Chatty Guy. Chatty Guy gets on our collective nerves by engaging the cashier in conversation. How were the holidays? We did this and we did that. We talked to this guy and we met that guy. We expected better weather. We hope this year will be better than last, and let me tell you that –

ARRRGHHH!

The foregoing expression is normally emitted in unison by the rest of the queue, just before we start hurling insults and frozen peas at Chatty Guy. I am always amazed that so few queue-related incidents of violence are reported to the police.

To avoid all this, I have decided to shop once a month at 03:50 in the morning at some all night supermarket. At least I will be too sleepy to be annoyed when everyone else comes to the same conclusion.

Fooling the System

You cannot defeat the System.

With the need to re-provision, I set out to a local and con-spicuously Unnamed Supermarket (let's call it "Mini"). I went through the traditional strolling of the aisles, pulling the nev-er changing assortment of comestibles and detersives from the never changing assortment on the shelves, and arrived in front of the Prepared Foods counter.

This is the home of the lazy home economist. We look at the prepared foods, knowing that the cooks at "Mini" go through rigorous training for at least 15 minutes before getting the job, and we weigh the benefits of food poisoning against our inher-ent laziness. Laziness usually wins in my case.

I ordered some different foods, including something from a vat that looked like stew but was probably more accurately called Goop, and made my way to the check-out counters. The per-son manning the cash register flew through my bar codes with deft alacrity, tossing the breakable and bruiseable items crash-ing down at the other end of the counter, while I scrambled to catch them mid-air.

Then she arrived at the Goop. She ran the bar-code three times until she discovered that there was no bar code. She called the Supervisor who arrived and spirited the Goop back to the pre-pared foods department to codify it. When he returned, he had a grave look on his face.

"You cannot buy this," he said.

What? There is a full vat of this Goop back there, and they have been doling it out to as many of us consumer idiots intrepid enough to try it. But, as I was told, it has no price entered in the System. So you cannot buy it, he repeated.

Now, determined to have my Goop, I argued my point, saying that if it was on display and given to me on request, and if this "Mini" (I looked around) is *actually* a supermarket, then I really should be able to buy it. No? The supervisor looked grave again. Or maybe just bored. It is hard to tell.

Sensing that I was not leaving without my Goop, he disappeared again. When he returned, he came back with three items that I did not want. Since "Goop" has no bar code, he said, he will run these three items, whose total price is the same as Goop apparently, onto my bill. That way, I suppose, we fool the System, and I get my Goop.

Although I am still not sure who won that round, I left the supermarket with one conclusion: fear of upsetting the System outweighs the urge to commit bad customer service.

This knowledge of the existence of a Higher Power (i.e., the System) is somehow reassuring.

How to Get New Clients in a Competitive Environment

A Play in One Act

The following is a true story…

"I want to change from Telenor to VIP."

"Can I have your lična karta?"

I give my ID card.

"Wait just a moment," he said, and he went to the back of the shop.

15 minutes later.

"You can switch, but you cannot use our phones," he declared.

"I did not ask for one," I said.

"Because you are a foreigner you cannot have any of our phones."

"I don't want I phone."

"You cannot have one."

"Why?"

"Because you are a foreigner."

"Did you look at my *lična karta*? I have been here for 10 years, I have owned two companies here, I have a JMBG. Why can't I have a phone?"

He shrugged his shoulders.

"Is that an explanation?" I asked, getting steamed up. "Let me talk to the manager," I said.

"He's not here."

"Who did you go talk to in the back?"

"A colleague."

"Let me talk to him."

"He does not decide on this."

"Then why should I care what he told you?"

More shrugging.

"Where is the manager then?" I asked.

"He's not here."

"Call him."

He pretends to call someone. We wait. He does not look at me.

"He does not answer."

"Tell him he lost a customer today."

"Ok."

"Make sure he knows about this – or I will."

EPILOGUE

With a final shrug of his shoulders, he indicated to me and everyone standing in line behind me that he could not care less that he just turned away a potential client. Moreover, he lost me as a client for exactly the WRONG reasons – I never wanted a 1 dinar phone from him or a two year contract, or anything. But he insisted so much on the fact that I could NOT have it that I could not, in good conscience, do further business with him.

Tonight he will go home and never think about this. In six months when VIP lays him off because the number of clients starts to decline, he will not wonder what his part in this story was.

He will just shrug his shoulders.

Fairy Tale Endings

It is the stuff of urban legends.

Sitting on the bus, pressing my neighbor's knee assertively back to his own seat as he attempted to sprawl across mine, thinking to myself why does everything have to be a challenge in this country – did he really think his passive-aggressive posture would keep the seat next to him free on the crowded 27E, I was visited by the Epiphany of Justice.

A ticket inspector, evil minion of the unaccountable BusPlus organization, approached. I withdrew my ticket for presentation. My carbuncular bus companion had none. I admit to smiling with thinly veiled Schadenfreude.

"Tickets."

"I don't have one," he said.

After an eye-ball standoff, the inspector said: "Next time."

I touched the inspector's blue sleeve as she turned to go.

"Give me 72 dinars, please," I said.

"Eh?"

"You let this guy ride for free, didn't you?"

"Ok, but…"

"I paid 72 dinars for a ticket. Didn't I?"

"Yes…"

"If this guy rides free, why should I pay?"

Silence.

"You owe me 72 dinars. 70 is ok." She started to move away from me. I held her sleeve.

"Did anyone else pay for a ticket?" I asked around the bus. A few hands went up. My bus companion was probably devising ways to kill me with his bare hands, but I did not look at him.

"You owe all these people 72 dinars. Each."

A riotous din of voices arose. People got to their feet, waving their tickets. Suddenly the Exalted Director of BusPlus appeared on the bus. He raised a great hairy hand and all of our tickets turned into gold. The timid inspector beamed radiantly. Laughter filled the crowded bus.

My bus companion was appointed Chief Inspector.

It is a funny thing, the imagination. This whole scene transpired in a flash. As it happens, no inspector came. No sleeves were tugged. No glorious reversal of circumstances ensued. That would make a fairy tale ending.

The reality is quite different from this little Walter Mitty fantasy. In reality we know that rules are applied unevenly, and the punishments are meted out randomly. The sad truth is that if the inspector had actually shown up in paragraph three, my companion would probably have gotten away with it, and I would be left muttering to myself about injustice. And, aside from ranting about it in the media, what can be done about it?

Maybe a little more sleeve tugging is in order.

Pedestrian Licensing

Should there not be a Code of the Road for pedestrians?

Following the demise of my automotive transport, I find my-self increasingly pounding the streets like a beat cop, walking along the sidewalks of Belgrade (when no one has parked upon them), through parks (when the packs of vicious dogs permit), along the closed pedestrian streets (dodging the signature-seekers and theatre-pass hawkers), and generally navigating the urban ebb and flow.

But the life of a pedestrian is neither foot loose nor fancy free.

As a driver, pedestrians were often the enemy. They dart across traffic. They bounce into the middle of a road whenever they please. They deliberately slow down to an indolent sashay on the crosswalks, asserting their rights not to be run over in so doing. Behind the wheel, all manner of expletives could be seen to be mouthed as I suffered their indignities. The enemy was implacable.

Now as a walker, I begin to understand the rhyme and reason. Drivers must learn the Rules. They are forced to know how to conduct themselves in traffic so as to cause the least amount of death and carnage in their daily lives. Pedestrians have no such restrictions. Generally it is known what they *should* do – and I have actually paid a fine for jay-walking across Makedonska, so the rules do exist – but in practice, the pedestrian is a lawless walker.

The group of three friends, for example, huddled together and laughing, taking one or two steps per minute, blocking the entire sidewalk behind them. When you are behind these three, you are forced either to slow down to their lackadaisical stroll or muscle-up and push past them. Pedestrians have no horns to honk. Maybe this would be a useful innovation.

And another thing. What about the escalators and moving walkways? People will step onto them and come to a complete stop, leaning on the handrails (which always move a little faster than the steps), and adopting poses of complete relaxation. Do these people think it is a ride? Is this Luna Park? I seem to remember that you should keep to the right on escalators if you do not intend to move your feet on them, thus allowing people to get by you on their way up or down. But if you are trying move, the withering looks of righteous indignation you will get as you try to nudge them out of the way are deadly.

"How dare he?" they humph.

I submit that there should be a license for pedestrians. They would have to learn to keep right, not to block traffic, to signal before walking straight into your path. The same license could be used for driving shopping carts in the supermarket.

In the meantime, I think I will start carrying a fog horn with me in my walking. The blast will certainly clear the path, even if some people end up jumping into traffic to avoid me.

Limited Choice

NEW YORK – Unbelievably, the idea of coming back home to Belgrade is now very appealing.

In Belgrade, if I want to buy toothpaste, I know where to go. I know I will have a certain limited amount of choice, I will choose, and I will go. In New York, where I have been for the past ten days, when I want to buy toothpaste, there are eighteen million places, that sell two hundred and fifty million different kinds with as many different prices and packages and deals available.

And I do not know where to start.

New York, as I have come to realize, is like going to a restaurant where the menu is the size of the Encyclopaedia Britannica, and you have seven minutes to choose, eat, and pay. It would take me more than a week just to decide, more or less, from which section to choose, let alone come to a conclusion about the specific dish.

I have spent a great deal of time over the years complaining about a lack of consumer choice in Belgrade. I have bemoaned that some things are not available to buy, that consumers are satisfied with the limitations like Plato's cave-dwellers, and that customer service is an unknown animal in the Belgrade menagerie.

But no more. After spending a week running back and forth over miles of concrete, searching for the perfect this and that, I understand that the amount of choice is just overwhelming. I KNOW already what kind of toothpaste I want to buy anyway – why do I spend hours searching and comparing and looking further to make sure that the other 249,999,999 other kinds are at least a little inferior to my original choice? The information comes at the cost of long days and tired legs.

New York is an amazing place. Everything, literally, is here. And everyone, literally, is pounding the streets with me as I try to fill a shopping list. The difference may be that many New Yorkers know where to go and have automatically filtered out the millions of alternatives. As a visitor, I cannot yet do that. My choice would be to stay here and study the question in depth. After six or seven years, I could probably accomplish a shopping list in fewer than four hours.

In a couple of days, I will return to the White City on the Danube and resume my life among the limited choices. In New York, if I do not see something I want to buy, it is because I do not know where it is – but I can be sure that it is here, somewhere, in the sprawling American Metropolis. In Belgrade, if I do not see something immediately that it probably does not exist – and I can go home knowing that I have done my best. Grumbling, maybe, but nevertheless with a degree of closure.

There is a distinct advantage to having extremely limited choices. At the very least, the choosing will not kill you.

The Retail Guard

The enemy is implacable, relentless.

When shopping for toys (*toys!*), I experienced a kind of outrage that very rarely plagues me. My curmudgeonly nature causes me to grumble and complain a lot and often, but very rarely does something, some behavior, drive me to the edge of tolerance. Toy shopping at Dexy Co. (and I name them so as not to indict an entire industry) has approached this threshold.

I walked into the store with my son, as we are wont to do, with an idea of browsing. My view on the myriad ranks of over-priced and over-specific toys available in Dexy and elsewhere is that they are rarely worth the prices asked. A toy's lifespan is measured in imagination-engagement, and a Spiderman figure which shoots webs at Venom serves its purpose in 7.23 minutes and is quickly abandoned thereafter. But the imagination is al-so sparked by viewing the shelves and seeing what is available.

As soon as we arrived at one particular aisle, an employee sta-tioned itself next to us. Standing still, watching, and fewer than three meters from us. The employee (although I think *soldier* would be a better appellation) It did not offer assistance. It did not open with the *Izvolite* Gambit, challenging our right to be in the store in the first place if we do not already know exact-ly what we want. It merely stationed itself next to us, intent on preventing us, the Implacable Enemy, from stealing.

The enemy is implacable, it is relentless.

Feeling under unwarranted scrutiny, I accosted it. I asked if we were ALLOWED to view the display of toys. Yes, it said. I asked if we were doing something WRONG. No, it said. So what are you doing here? It is my job, it said.

I raised my voice and told it to back away, to go stand some-where else. I told it that it was making me feel uncomfortable. Clearly, it was not expecting my reaction and it drifted a few aisles away, looking offended. We continued our browsing and, inevitably, stumbled upon something that absolutely had to be bought to ensure the continued happiness of my son. I paid, and we left.

But the unspoken accusation of the Toy Soldier stayed with me. The principle of the thing is the problem. Its duty was to stay close to us. It operates on the assumption that ALL shoppers are potential criminals and that they would, left to their own unsupervised devices, rob the store blind. The assumption of malevolent intent is the stone in my shoe.

This incident happened several weeks ago. It recurred, however, yesterday, and my response was not to accost and frighten the Toy Soldier again (it was a new one) but I could not remain in the store. The tactic of self-protection engaged by Dexy Co. has put an end to my continued custom – I will not be returning there to suffer the ignominy of their distrust and suspicion.

Shoplifting, I admit, is a problem for all retail. Some handle it by cameras and general vigilance. Most shops have electronic barriers that prevent people from walking out with ill-gotten gains. I cannot fault a shop for wanting to prevent that kind of inevitable crime. But the policy of stationing soldiers to guard the goods from shoppers crosses a line. I have seen this elsewhere, e.g., Vero supermarkets, and it always has the same effect on me.

The soldiers cannot engage an enemy which does not appear for the battle. The effect is that I take my business elsewhere.

Summer Flea Marketing

If it is nowhere to be found, conventional wisdom tells us, then it may not exist. Conventional wisdom used to tell us that if it is nowhere to be found it might be at the flea market. I think this is no longer true.

I just spent three days and nights billeted at Buvljak, the flea market next to Vero in New Belgrade, and I have come away with the following inventory: One t-shirt, a plastic box with no apparent function, one CD of dubious and unnamable origin, a bread box, four unasserted pillows, a toilet seat, and a hub cap. None of these items, of course are on my list. And none of the items on my list are checked as being obtained.

Ok. I was only there for about 50 minutes, but it felt longer.

The flea market used to be the place to go to find the thing that your imagination conjured up and told you that you needed. It could be a triangular bamboo table, a purple spotted bedcover, or a length of copper cable. Whatever it was, somehow someone at the flea market had six of them.

These days, however, even Buvljak has become as homogenous as the Delta Citizens or Ušćean shops. There are millions of t-shirts which all look the same, a pair of myriad replicated sweat socks with the Nike logo facing the wrong way. Every clothing shop has the same cargo pocket pants, the same plaid shirts, and the same frumpy dresses. It does not take long as you walk down the narrows alleyways for the goods and people to meld and blur into one. It is like spending more than two hours in the Louvre, eventually all the paintings look like the Mona Lisa.

In fact, I saw a Mona Lisa clock at Buvljak today. In 17 different places.

I often wonder what goes through the minds of the people who spend all day in the stalls watching people like me stumble past. We onlookers have dazed expressions, walk too fast to notice much and too slowly to seem purposeful. If we have no bags in our hands, we are almost invisible. If we have at least one purchase, then we are punters and they engage you in riveting dialogue, like "what do you want?"

But that is the point. If you know what you want, you are in the wrong place. If you go to the flea market and have a specific thing in mind, you will NEVER find it. And you come back with a t-shirt, a plastic box with no apparent function, one CD of dubious and unnamable origin, a bread box, four unasserted pillows, a toilet seat, and a hub cap. The point of going there now is to see what you discover. And due to the homogenization of choice, you only need to randomly sample a few stalls to know what's out there.

But another mystery of the flea market is that even though I have these EXACT SAME THOUGHTS every time I go, I cannot stop myself from going back soon after. There is something magic about the idea of the flea market which suggests that everything imaginable and not is there waiting for me. This time, however, I decided to commit my experience to a blog and prevent myself from recidivism. I will NOT go back there, and if the urge is too strong, I will reread these words to remind me. I will display my hub cap and toilet seat prominently in my home as a memento.

And then I will drive off to Pančevo.

Tlön, Uqbar, Orbis Tertius

Since moving into our stately new offices in Sarajevksa, I have had one nagging problem: my books keep falling down.

Stubbornly persistent, I line them up on my desk and, after an interval ranging between 5 minutes and 2 days, they all slide down onto the floor with an inelegant but highly eloquent series of thuds.

Inspiration, ever my traveling companion, suggested to me that what I needed were Book-Ends. Simple pieces of plastic, metal, or wood, they are placed strategically at the polar extremes of a small row of books (i.e, on my desk). The weight of the books firmly anchors the books in place and no series of thuds ever ensues after their application. Quite a marvelously simple invention, I think.

I have known book-ends all of my life. My father's multifarious collection of art books was book-ended into regimental alignment; my mother's record albums (see Wikipedia: "Album" for those readers born after 1980) maintained standard perpendicular formation by means of book-ends. I had them in high school. I knew them in college. In short, I count on the knowledge of their physical existence.

That is, I counted on this fact until now.

As far as I can tell, and I have made a special study of this phenomenon, THERE ARE NO BOOK-ENDS IN SERBIA. This, naturally, brings me to a choice of several ontological conclusions: a) Serbian books do not fall down; b) gravity is only selectively applied in the Balkans; c) Serbian bookshelves are completely filled (no half rows requiring a book-end); d) my understanding of existence *per se* has become tenuous and untrustworthy.

Of this, only d) seems to conform to other patterns in My Life in Belgrade (an unpublished book consisting of pages which do not yet exist). Often have I tried to find certain objects or commodities in Belgrade which so far have eluded my grasp. Of these objects, more might be said at another time (although I am grateful to my friend Dan for causing Hellmann's Mayonnaise to materialize on the shelves of grocery stores).

Existence is a knotty problem: if only I am aware of the substance of book-ends, can they be said to exist?

Jorge Luis Borges wrote about material objects that were willed into existence by thought. He called them "hronin." Better still, he also spoke of objects which came into being through sheer hope: "Ur."

In my mind, I fashion an image of the two L-shaped pieces of plastic which I need to hold up my books. I then transport that image into a shop. I enter the shop and ask about book- ends. No dice.

The nature of existence is quite fragile. I am much less certain today that book-ends ever existed at all. I am no longer sure if my father actually just stacked his books in a pile in the corner. The quizzical looks and raised eyebrows which greet my constant search for book- ends – and I am sure that I have seen 100 shops by now – make me question all of my initial assumptions about what IS and what IS NOT real. It is all very disconcerting.

And now, having said all of this, I can no longer remember where I parked my unicorn.

CONSUMERS &
OTHER ANIMALS

UnREAL POLITIK

Looking for fun and adventure?
Want to lie to everyone and get paid for it?
Would you like to expose yourself to public ridicule
and rage against the media?

Make a difference – become a politician!

We can dress them up, give them fancy speeches to proclaim, and plaster their faces over every available public surface, but the subspecies *homo politicus,* or "Lying Man", is the same all over the world.

In this section, you will see a minister of foreign affairs, a president, an interior minister, and giraffe-dealing local mayor – the names will mean something to you if you were living in Serbia in the early part of this millennium, but if you weren't I have an important message for you:

You did not miss too much.

Some of these guys continue to entertain us with their antics, some have passed into obscurity, and others still are hanging around the sidelines ready to Look Stupid for their Country as soon as they get the chance.

NOTE: I would like to it be said, before you launch into reading, that I hold each person alluded to or mentioned here with the DEEPEST OF ALL POSSIBLE RESPECT that is due any member of the political caste. All of it.

Please forward your cards and letters in care of Republic Correctional Institution, Cellblock D. Last on the left.

Political Animals

September is now upon us. We are getting back to work after a long and protracted holiday (even if we did not take one, everyone else seems to have done so). Streets are busier. Shops are crowding up slowly again. Supermarkets may even begin to stock the shelves once more. The fall season – in a way very different from the burgeoning of spring – is all about new beginnings. Schemes hatched on the beach will be either evaluated or binned. Board rooms are being dusted down and ready to contain corporate posteriors once again.

And it is high time to think about politics.

Elections are coming again and the campaign clamor is about to begin clamoring for our attention. We have the usual suspects to root for and to despise – depending on which side of the fence toward which we wobble. Same old song and dance. What is needed is something to stir the pot.

With this in mind, I am accepting nominations to run for President of Serbia.

Presidential elections are a little bit further away (although I have no idea when further away will happen), so there is enough time to establish the SSS (Stranka Stranaca Srbije), constitute its board, and start pasting up the billboards.

Among my priorities, as a candidate, is to have a LIST OF PRIORITIES. This seems to get very little play here – no need for policy positions, platforms, prospectuses, and programs: we usually elect on personalities. Normally, the vote is *against* the rest of the personalities and not for the remaining one or two.

The SSS Platform

- Free parking for SSS members
- State sinecures for all of my friends, including Facebook friends
- Support for the Independent Republic of Palilula
- Earmarked taxes

- Institutionalized corruption (i.e., VAT redemptions on bribery)
- Other Important Stuff

While Other Important Stuff covers a multitude of sins, the idea of the Independent Republic of Palilula is a winner. We will declare independence on a Tuesday afternoon, say, apply for EU funding and USAID donations for institution building, be coy with NATO, and set up an independent state-within-a state along the lines of Vatican City, with me as Pope, by the end of the week.

Not to stick too closely to ceremony, my humble title will be His Serene Eminence the Maharishi of Palilula.

We will erect toll booths on the Pančevo Bridge to help revenue streams, charge admission to Tašmajdan Park, and levy traffic congestion fees for non-Palilula residents travelling our streets. We will also have to amend the constitution to allow the maharishi to hold the office of president concurrently.

In return, IRP citizens will be offered visa-free travel to the rest of Belgrade, a new sticker for their cars (the license plates will come later), and our own currency, the IRP Tolar which will be pegged to the Chinese yuan. We, in Palilula, know which way the wind is blowing….

Nominations may be submitted through this blog, by public declarations on street corners (bring your own soap box), or by the writing on the walls.

Good luck to all!

Dog Watching for Democracy

There are about twelve dogs outside my window, more or less.

If you close your eyes and listen, there might be five hundred. No one loves these dogs. They are loud, abrasive, and harbor a particular dislike for passing cars. The dogs live in a large dirt bottomed lot, replete with hills and valleys and studded with protruding atramental re-bar in the Non-Operational Construction Area for Suspended Housing (NO- CASH) – an open field/apartment block in transition. A perfect place for our twelve neighborhood dogs.

The space they occupy bothers no one. There is no overt sign of heavy machinery coming to finish creating a building out of the embedded concrete columns which were pile-driven into the ground every day from 6 am to 11 pm two years ago. The space is a no-man's-land where our twelve dogs have developed a microcosmic civilization.

No one has actually counted these dogs, but twelve appears to be a propitious number for them. The number brings to mind scenes of the last supper, the hours of the clock, the months of the year, the signs of the zodiac, and the stations of the Moon and of the Sun.

Twelve dogs.

The untrained eye cannot distinguish among them – they are "dogs." Given a little effort, if you can find someone other than myself who will take the time to do so, a person might venture that one dog is bigger, one dog is louder, one dog less socialized, one scruffier. The dogs ALL appear to be the leader. This does not happen at the same time, but (again you have to WANT to find this out) there is a discernable, if syncopated, rhythm for change-in-command in this group of twelve dogs. Within a five minute interval, a leader may have been installed and overthrown eight times – with the Big Dog getting more than his fair share of turns at bat.

This means that if I go look out my window at odd intervals during the day, I will see a new powerscape nearly every time.

Each glance reveals a subtle or shocking reordering of the gears and levels that indicate Power within this circle of twelve. I have yet to determine the real criteria for mounting a coup-d'état, what qualifies a leader in this group, which are the backdoor-bargainers and which are the populists. As the group is completely self-contained, each dog is simultaneously constituent, candidate, incumbent, and contender.

It is likewise unclear to me what constitutes a successful regime for a leader. From the outside (read *human*) point of view, each configuration is equally cantankerous, cacophonic, and consternating – although I have never felt fear of direct assault by the group, I have often worried about *bavures*, accidental overspills of canine exuberance.

But to these twelve dogs, the power struggle is clear and present. No matter what role they are playing at whatever moment, the next move is being planned – and while this hatching of plots is going on, perhaps another leader has been toppled again. It is a continual motion machine wherein the status quo is a measure of change.

I must say that I find the yipping and yapping of these twelve dogs a constant annoyance. I often find myself wishing for, say, a passing crash of rhinoceroses to migrate into the NO-CASH zone and replace them. For their part, I am fairly certain that the dogs are unaware of the human population encroaching around them. They are far too concerned with their internal affairs to waste any time contemplating their place in the Universe.

I should also say that I do not usually spend so much time thinking about their doings. From time to time, events in our world lend themselves to analogy and metaphor. The all-too-human squabbling that we read about in our papers sometimes leads to a fleeting indulgence in anthropomorphism.

My hope is that as soon as we have a new government, most of the barking will subside.

Foreign Minister

There is probably something wrong with my phone.

As soon as the announcement came last month that foreigners were wanted in the new flip-flopped Serbian government, I was on alert. Surely the call would come from Aleksandar Vučić asking me to take over a few portfolios. Not too many, enough to keep me occupied a couple days a week.

But the call never came. I should get my phone serviced.

You can understand my surprise. After all, I have always demonstrated the GREATEST respect for the leaders who have navigated the transition with the grim determination of a lemon peel floating down the Danube. The archives of this blog demonstrate my UNWAVERING support and encouragement to boneheaded decisions, wild ideas and public statements, and the generally farcical behavior which constitutes the backbone (or lack thereof) of a career in the Serbian government.

After all, without it, I would have nothing to write about.

In retrospect, I suppose my chances were hampered by a few different factors. The finance post was closed to me because I have already passed through puberty. The position of high advisor was also nixed since I have never been accused of or brought up on charges for prostitution or pimping (although I do speak French).

Culture would have been a nice portfolio, I suppose, but I do not have enough hair.

The idea of opening the ministerial field to foreigners was an interesting play, however. A lot of us foreigners who have been in Belgrade for much longer than would seem immediately necessary were given pause to speculate and wonder. We, the foreign residents of Belgrade, constitute a disenfranchised group – we cannot vote, we cannot get one of the cheap phones that VIP offers, and we are continually overcharged for everything from taxis to potatoes. We could even become a political party or qualify for European inclusion projects.

Having a foreigner in charge would also have been a great fall-back position for Mr. Vučić

– we make the unpopular moves, and he could shrug his shoulders and say, "You know, he's a foreigner, he's not from here, he doesn't get it." The other advantage of having a non-native minister is that official translators could become the new policy shapers and king-makers.

In the end, none of the nine new guys are even remotely foreign. The invitation to join the government turned out to be an empty promise. We got all geared up, shuffling our schedules to make room for the occasional cabinet meeting, composed wish-lists of laws to change, picked out countries against whom to wage war, and bought a new suit or two – and then nothing.

It is like being uninvited to a birthday party. What do you do with the gifts you intended to bring?

Stone Squeezing

There are two rules about squeezing blood from a stone. First: it does not work. Second: apply enough pressure and the stone will eventually crumble. Work gloves are recommended.

With the spate of price increases here and there of excises and specific taxes which was landed on our collective heads in Serbia this week – cigarettes, bus tickets, fuel, heating costs, and VAT which affects almost everything else – the government is showing us that they are fresh out of fresh ideas.

Ironically, when the government overspends (as they are doing consistently), the great thinkers in charge of the Brilliant Ideas Department think that they can just off-load this kind of recklessness onto the consumers. Problem solved! Not enough money? More taxes!

Easy peasy.

Sadly, when the CONSUMER overspends, we are left to squeeze the stones. For the most part, in this highly regulated and boisterously bureaucratic society, we are not allowed to overspend. But if the consumer *does* manage to overspend his budget, he is left out in the cold. He is thrown off the bus. He is threatened with sanctions; he may be jailed; or he may just be beaten up by disgruntled creditors.

Just as a side note, I would like to point out that we live in a Consumer Society. This means, essentially, that the consumer is the driving force behind everything. The things we build and the services we offer are ultimately paid for by the consumer. When he is out of money, then the system should go offline.

But now, rather than coming with innovation and good ideas to fuel the consumer machine (i.e., put more money in the consumers' pockets so they go out and spend and keep the wheels of commerce spinning), we do the opposite. We decide that it is Wise to extract more money from the consumer while expecting him to keep our coveted system turning...

Hm.

As to raising taxes, let's be honest with ourselves. This will AL-WAYS happen. It is the nature of taxes to go up. But I think we should expect a little more bang for our buck. If the prices of bus tickets go up, we should expect better service, not just a bigger congregation of BusPlus inspectors in their branded polo shirts haunting the bus stops.

The VAT hike is the most ironic of all. Bigger Value Added Tax makes everything costlier, but what value has been increased proportionately? It is pure fantasy.

The pressure is building in the boiler. As a consumer, I feel affronted to live in a country where the average earnings do not cover the average consumer grocery bill and then to hear our elected officials (i.e., *chosen by the people*) tell us that the best way out of the crisis is to make the cash-strapped Serbian public pay for it.

Something is wrong, Prince John. The peasants are revolting.

There are not enough jobs. There is not enough industry. There are not enough foreign investors. There is not enough money. Does anyone REALLY think that the people are hoarding enough dinars in their respective mattresses (bought on credit, by the way) to finance the recovery?

I apologize if this blog has turned into a rant, but I think it is time for people to be angry about all this. The policy of squeezing stones will eventually leave us a pile of gravel.

The Silence...

Pity the poor media consumer in Serbia! For the next 48 hours, we have lost our daily bread of electioneering, promises, baby-kissing, lovely hand-knit sweaters (providing the coveted Man-of-the-People causal look), dramatic camera angles, flag-waving, and – of course – rampant speculation about who plans to get in bed with whom after the electoral chips have all fallen.

The news programs will have to contain (egad!) NEWS, reminding us that while we have all been wondering about what Serbia will become, the cold shower of what Serbia actually IS is still out there on our doorsteps.

Hopes and dreams, step aside please!

But little did we realize that the famous election silence is actually part of a hugely CUNNING PLAN. As the hours of silence tick away until we go out to tick our ballots, the memory of the electioneering and campaigns rapidly begins to fade. By the time Sunday rolls around, we will all have forgotten which of the 20 candidates said what to whom. The candidates, as usual and as part of their job descriptions, have all made promises and made bold statements which would all benefit from a little mnemonic fuzziness so that when the winners and the losers are all sorted out, there will be ample room for maneuvering and explaining why everything will pretty much be the same.

After the elections (and after the various shenanigans of political horse-trading in creating the next government), the same questions will remain unanswered. We will still wonder about getting into the EU. We will still wait to see our salaries match the cost of living. We will still be asked about cooperation with The Hague. And, let's not forget the upcoming ex-cathedra proclamations of Pope Serge Brammertz. The incoming government, in short, will have the same To Do List as the outgoing one – even if the names and faces are changed.

During the election period, however, we have been able to sleep through these issues, hypnotized as we were by the flags and the sweaters. Now it is time for The Silence to reign, the fog of forgetfulness to roll in over the slogans.

Ironically, although we are generously given 48 hours to forget, I think 20 minutes might have done the trick.

Empathy Pains

"If I weren't the president of the republic, maybe I would be dissatisfied and embittered too." So said Boris Tadić this week, reminding us of our obligation to vote and thereby give voice to our dissatisfaction and bitterness that we all feel because we are not president of the republic.

Hm…

I was reminded by one reader that I should pay attention to the CONTEXT in which this enormity was stated, that perhaps I was overreacting to something misquoted, misconstrued, or misplaced and out of context. But I am sorry: the sentence is utterly indefensible.

Never mind that I cannot vote here – there are still a few semantic bones to be picked in this bit of presidential glibness. The implication is very clear that the president IS indeed satisfied and not bitter because he is president. What other way is there to read this?

By extension, he implies that maybe having a cool job (like being president of the republic for example) staves off dissatisfaction and bitterness. In that case, who cares if we vote or not?

Another bit of gristle in the brisket: the president tells us to vote (and not to boycott upcoming elections) because in so doing we can speak our truth to their power. But what if we vote for someone else, Mr. President? This will certainly become a serious impediment to your satisfaction, while not necessarily decreasing the general bitterness. After all, only one of us gets to be president of the republic.

One can only assume that the president was attempting to demonstrate his deep empathy with the predicament of the Serbian people over which he has presided for the past several years and hopes to continue into the Putinesque future. But he did not express empathy, really. He said MAYBE he would be bitter. MAYBE he would be dissatisfied.

Thank you, O Leader, for very nearly feeling our pain.

The Story of Vook
and the Great Big Whale

Now, a long time ago, in beginning of the Age of Information, there lived a boy named Vook. He had a nice shiny suit of clothes, always brushed his teeth before bed, and was very proud of the things that he could say.

Everyone across the land would smile and beam when they heard him speak. He could say "no" when most folk would have said "yes." He would not just play with anyone – and he would tell them the reasons. Vook was the apple of his Papa B's eye. Papa B would send him out into the world and ask him what he saw. And Vook, proud and pleased, would come back and tell him all about it.

But Vook was a very stubborn boy and would not change his mind once it was set. If people asked him, he would sometimes say: "I don't wanna" and hold his breath. Papa B told him his stubborn head would one day get into trouble, but Vook would not listen.

Now one day, Vook, while traveling far and wide, came across a Great Big Whale. The Whale was very large and, above the sea, the skies were filled with little bluebirds tweeting and chirping above the waters where the Whale would swim. Sometimes the birds would lift the Great Big Whale out of the water by little strings held in their beaks. When that happened, you knew something very important was happening.

Vook stopped to listen to the birds. They chirped and tweeted and, all of a sudden, Vook thought he heard them tweet his name! He thought they were saying things about him. He thought they were laughing at him and his shiny suit and white teeth. Vook turned his boat around and ran back home.

When he arrived back home, he called all the whale hunters of the land to seek out the Great Big Whale.

And he summoned the hunters to take aim at the birds. He said this Great Big Whale and some of its many birds where "unpleasant" and he decided to take out the bad ones.

The birds, once they heard, began to follow Vook around. They asked him what he was doing. They asked why he hated them so. They wanted him to answer. But Vook said, "I don't wanna," and did not tell. He would not talk with any of the birds.

When Papa B heard what little Vook was doing, he called him over. "What are you doing to these birds?" he asked. "These birds seem little but they are very powerful, and they are very loud, and there are too many of them."

"I will stop them," Vook blustered. "They are mean to me."

Vook did not know that the birds were very friendly with the world's gentle winds. He did not know that their voices carried from one side of the earth to the other upon the winds, and that once they began to chirp, no one could silence them for long.

But Papa B wanted the Great Big Whale to be on his side. He did not want little Vook to bother it and poke it with sticks. "You may go after the birds and whale," he said, "but if you anger the Great Big Whale, I will let it swallow you up."

And Vook did not wanna. He stood by the sea in his shiny suit, holding Papa B's suit of armor, and shook his fist at the sea and the birds and the Great Big Whale. But he was very, very quiet. He did not say a word.

And the birds tweeted and chirped and flew away, leaving only the sound of their voices behind.

The Hunger

If I stopped eating for two days, most people would call it a DI-ET.

Toma Nikolić, after what seems to be 48 hours of hunger strik-ing (although I cannot be sure of the accuracy of media reports) in an attempt to bring about early elections in Serbia, has been hospitalized.

Even Dr. Atkins says that you need at least three days before the body starts feeling the effects of hunger.

With all due respect to the Mahatma, I just do not get the polit-ical savvy behind the hunger strike. It is the equivalent of a child holding its breath until his parents buy him a pony. I looked up a few examples of 'successful' hunger strikes and found, aside from Gandhi, almost no positive outcomes. Gandhi was butt-ing heads with the British Empire and trying to bring attention to the plight of subjugated Indians to the world. Toma, on the other hand, is butting heads with the Serbian electorate, a few million voters.

I guess Toma's party ran out of arguments. They have been vo-ciferously screaming and shouting for early elections for the past few weeks, culminating in a mass rally in Belgrade on Saturday. When nothing else worked, the idea of a hunger strike must have seemed just too cool to ignore. We will stop eating! Great idea!

[As a side note, we in Belgrade began a Traffic Strike on Satur-day (reinforced on Sunday by the marathon) and left our cars at home for most of the weekend since the city was not navigable.]

The thing about the hunger strike that bugs me is that it con-tains no rational argument or reasoning.

Basically the Hunger Striker is placing the butt of a very, very slow revolver to his temple and telling us that unless we give in to his demands he will commit suicide. I think we get it. He wants elections now. But failing that: death? I am not sure history will record this favorably. I am not even sure if history will record it at all…

It will be interesting to see how the ruling coalition deals with this. If they give in, they lose all the way around – their positions, their sense of dignity, and their backbones will all be unceremoniously trash-heaped out back behind the Serbian parliament. If they hang tough, people will call them inhuman monsters. And what about Toma? Will he allow the hunger to kill him?

The disproportion of this hunger strike is the thing. On the one hand, the stakes are an election – we have them all the time here. Most pollsters show that no matter when we have elections Toma's party will fare better than the others. So what is the hurry? I wonder. On the other hand, the crisis level of Toma's hunger strike seems a little exaggerated as well. Two days? The autumn of 1924, Gandhi was on a hunger strike for three weeks in protest. But in 1933, he did a 21 day fast of purification for the benefit of himself alone. He trained for this. Did Toma?

Maybe I should go on a hunger strike until Toma ends his. At worst I will lose the extra five kilos that I have wanted to get rid of for awhile now.

I will start after breakfast….

The Hunger II: Endgame

One week later…

When hunger does not do the trick, let's eat then.

After a week of undue media attention – and, yes, ok, I am part of it regrettably – Toma has come back to the dinner table, seeing that no one else was going to show up at the negotiating table. The spin seems to be that he has called attention to the need for Serbia to move forward. On to the main course, as it were…

A week earlier, Toma was ready to starve himself to death rather than not get early elections. This week, after the tempting paschal aromas of sarma and proja and pasulj prebranac wafted into his hospital room, he substituted "moving forward" for "early elections" as a good reason to stop the hunger strike.

Philosophers and theologians alike agree that that mankind tends to move forward no matter what stupid things we do; so the new endgame seems ok.

Given that many people were nearing the end of their quadragesimal fasting last week, the timing seems pretty good. I am surprised the Patriarch did not see it that way.

I have to admit that I am a little disappointed in the denouement of this gastronomic drama. I had expected that Toma might hold on a little longer than eight days and really make his opponents shift uncomfortably in their eats over the Easter feast. Instead, he just gave up.

Life is less interesting than fiction. And please pass the proja.

Appropriate Mourning

Where does the line get drawn?

The passing of Patriarch Pavle, for whom all the respect paid to his memory was and is well deserved, allowed for some rather questionable decisions on the side of the government and media in Serbia. The government asked media to restrict itself to "appropriate" content during the declared official days of mourning. This, by itself, seems reasonable. Some channels on television did not transmit at all and replaced their programs with a blackened screen saying that it was because of the mourning period. Some announced changes in the programming schedule for the same reason.

Others, especially those controlled by the SBB Cable Monopolists, seem to have hired a crew of coin-flippers to make their decisions on Appropriateness. Moreover, instead of warning the public, they just took the censored channels off the air, leading many of us to fiddle for some time with the television's controls until we cottoned on. Personally, I blamed my five-year old son for playing with the remote control when I could not find the channels.

I have since apologized.

I looked for patterns in the choices. Why Fox Life, for example, and not Fox Crime? Is it because situation comedies are Bad and shows sympathizing serial killers and the mafia are Good? Why Croatian television and not Bosnian? Is it because many Croats are Catholics and might not choose to turn off the TV themselves – so SBB does it for them?

In all, SBB cancelled ten channels – music channels VH1, MTV, and Melos; regional channels HRT1 and 2 and OBN; and some others, including Fox Life, Atlas, DM Sat, and Fashion TV. Who was making these decisions?

It occurs to me that true mourning is spontaneous. The Republic of Serbia 'suggested' that companies give their employees a paid day off on Thursday, the day of the Patriarch's funeral. It was stipulated that the day be "paid." If anyone had come to me to ask for the day off out of respect for the mourning period, I am quite sure we would have given it. Nor would we have docked them the day's pay for doing it. But I am fairly certain of the fact that this would be the company's decision. The state has no business suggesting it to us. Many will mistake a suggestion for an instruction.

The government, as a major employer in Serbia, gave its people a free day – and this is even less appropriate than a private company. After all, the government is put in place (theoretically) by the voters of Serbia, not all of whom are Serbian Orthodox. It feels divisive, instantly making camps of Us and Them. "Us" comprise a clear majority in this fairly homogenous state – in 2002, it was estimated by the Statistics Bureau that some 84% of the population was Serbian Orthodox. But "Them," in which I also find myself along with Catholics, Buddhists, Muslims, Protestants, and every other non-Orthodox resident, still live here and represent about half a million people. Not counting Kosovo because that would bump it up to around 2.5 million people.

Us and Them.

It does not mean we should not join the mourning, but no one really has a choice in it either. Just like we did not have the choice to switch off the TV if we wanted to observe it. Being allowed the freedom to turn off gives people the chance to show genuine respect, but deciding for people is another story altogether. In the meantime, I have been told that porn and violence were readily available on TV during the mourning period anyway. The coin-flipping strategy seems to have left a few gaps.

Heads I win, Tails you lose.

Gonna Fly Now

The year was 1976.

A disenchanted American nation was ready to vote in a Georgia peanut farmer as president, to put away the hallucinogens which blurred out most of the late 60s and early 70s, to put away their anti-Vietnam War banners, and start over again. The morale of the US of A was lagging by defeat in Asia, humiliation in the White House, and the beginnings of recession and the Energy Crisis.

Enter the Italian Stallion: Rocky Balboa

Rocky, the film of the year, was the story of loser made good. Many people called it the embodiment of the American Dream. How a down and out Philadelphia boxer moves up the ranks to challenge and defeat the heavyweight champion of the world is the kind of rags to riches story which is "inspirational" and "quintessentially American."

Enter Toma Nikolić.

For his new radical party off-shoot, the Serb Progressive Party (SNS), Toma pulled out all the stops to do his first major rally in Belgrade. And as he walked into the hall, the music started to play. It was music that every middle-aged American in Serbia (me, James Lyon, and a couple of embassy guys) immediately felt reverberating in the Great American Nostalgia. The music was at the top of the US music charts in 1976 through 1977 and is still played whenever Great Feeling needs to be stirred. The theme from Rocky – "Gonna Fly Now."

Hm…

Now many may wonder how the assuredly rightist and allegedly ultra-rightist Toma could ever possibly choose fanfare music which is the personification of the American Dream. One might have expected to hear **Государственный гимн Российской Федерации** (the Hymn of the Russian Federation) or at least a little of the 1812 Overture of Tchaikovsky. That's a moving piece of non-Western aligned ideological music. Isn't it?

But Toma knows better. Music is a powerful subliminal motivator. And this is not the first time that he has looked across the Atlantic for his inspiration. I still remember listening to Vangelis, the Conquest of Paradise, used in the movie 1492, when Toma was running for president in 2004. I thought the choice was amazingly strong, but I could not exactly place where I heard it before. So I called the Serbian Radical Party to ask.

At first they thought I was joking. But then I was passed from apparatchik to secretary to assistant deputy someone or other who told me that it came from 1492.

"You mean the movie about Colombus discovering America?" "I dunno."

"Are you SURE?" I asked, a little taken aback. "*Da.*"

The ostensible and less-than-subtle message seems to be that Toma's "getting strong now" and he's "gonna fly now." The words seem to work with the ambition, but the overall effect – that he and Aca will go ten rounds with the opposition in parliament – seems a little… I don't know… *American*, if you see what I mean.

But these American movies nearly ALWAYS have a Happy Ending. I guess this could be Toma's point of difference.

Gotta fly now.

The Great Giraffe Caper

Brooding in his study, the Kingpin mused over his most recent ingenious plan. *What good is it to continually try to destroy Spiderman when he eludes my every effort? I must now turn my attention to a diversion…*he contemplated the thought with a wry smile on his face.

"I must have a giraffe," he concluded.

The Kingpin had always been a secret admirer of the elegant long-necked beasts, in stark contrast to his own squat frame and imposing bulk. But in order to obtain a giraffe, it would not be enough to buy one – he could buy a menagerie of giraffes if he were so inclined. He would have to turn it into something inscrutably interesting.

"By the time, I am finished they will be lining up to offer me giraffes. I will put my weight behind it and bestow my favors only on he who brings me the BEST giraffe."

With one phone call, the wheels were already beginning to spin. Toma had a crocodile, but only Voja came up with the coveted African *giraffa camelopardalis.*

Krkobabić had only asked for a turtle.

Dash for the Border

My babysitter has her bags packed.

One fine day, a couple of weeks ago, I heard the announcement that if the Radicals should win the upcoming presidential elections – i.e., Smiling Tommy Nik – that she was ready to pack up and leave the country.

Hm, I told her.

And I really did mean it. I thought, hm, where is she going to go? I thought, hm, if the protection of my son, who is alternatively Zorro, Spiderman, and Pachycephalosaurus, depending on his mood, was not enough for her, what else would be? And – I continued in my hmming – where did she think the next best refuge for her would be? Moreover, I hmmed, and I placed particularly poignant emphasis on the phoneme, *why*?

As an extraneous foreign unit, I know that my musings on the elections – and I have had the chance to muse about a great many of them in the five years that I have been here – are not extremely valuable. Moreover, I know that many of you who are reading my musings are probably not voters either. However, as I (we) will be subject to the whims of whatever regime is tipped for the Big Chair, as much as any voter, I am a concerned constituent.

AND because the outcome of the elections will directly determine whether I need to find a new babysitter or not, I am sure that I have at least one dog in this fight.

The first task that I needed to address was to determine was what she would do if SOMEONE ELSE were elected. As far as I am concerned, you need a contingency plan for all potential outcomes. For example, if Minister Čačak is elected, does she plan to leave Belgrade for the new Central Serbian capital? If she stays, does she plan for a new attitude toward infrastructure projects? If Boris stays, is it status quo? And what about Čeda or Milanka or Milutin Mrkonjić? The point is why do the Radicals get their own plan?

Problematically, it seems to me that every result of this race should force us to consider taking flight. The candidate could be an ultra-nationalist, an alleged criminal, a potato, a drug addict, a moll, or a Pachycephalosaurus (hypothetically speaking, of course), but it is clear now – as opposed to earlier presidential elections I have seen – that SOMEONE will be elected. When Someone is anointed with the ceremonial oils, Someone will have a policy agenda, and Someone will want to get a few things done right away – even if the first agenda item is to go on holiday.

Therefore I ask you, o guardian of my child, wherefore the almighty rush to the border for one man alone?

The other question I had hmmed about was the Why. I am struggling to comprehend the possible downside to babysitting under a Radical presidency. It is a puzzler to me. Maybe she has some SECRET INFORMATION about babysitting plans direct from undercover sources in Zemun. Does she think that Nik will be against the fair treatment of babysitters? Do the Radicals plan to institute a National Babysitting Plan? Will the continued existence of babysitters, under the NBP, be contingent on Euro-Atlantic integration? On Russian investment? On the status of Kosovo?

Clearly, my babysitter knows more than she is letting on.

From my point of view, it is hard to distinguish the possible changes which a new (or renewed) president will want to enforce regarding babysitting. The president's purview does not cover babysitting now, as far as I know. Any of the possible (hypothetical) candidates would have to push it through the cabinet and through the parliament. This is roughly comparable to pushing a large metallic object through a slab of granite by applied pressure from three finger-tips.

We are still a few weeks away from any possible exodus, but I will be monitoring the relative distance of my babysitter's bags to the door. Extraneous foreign unit that I am, I will not have much to say about babysitting policies. If she must really abscond to parts unknown and unradical, I will not stand in her flight path. I will, however, suggest she adopt a wait-and-see attitude.

After all, as long as she stays, she still has Spiderman on her side.

Severe Putin Watch

The weather in Belgrade today: sunny skies, highs in the mid to upper teens, and a high chance of Vladimir Putin, clearing by evening or overnight.

Back in Iowa, on winter mornings, we would listen to the radio to see if school was cancelled because of heavy snow. Later, in Saudi Arabia, we would wait to hear if school was cancelled because of unbearable heat or sandstorms. In Belgrade, however, we have another phenomenon which should cause the schools to close, stop all traffic in the city, and disrupt life in isolated incidents and pockets of local disturbances.

We get Foreign Dignitaries.

World leaders and heads of state whiz in and out of London nearly unnoticed. They land in Paris and depart before anyone knows it. In New York it is just another day when they are in town. But in Belgrade, the arrival of a world leader places us in suspended animation for the hours of his or her visits. The police close down streets all over the city – just in case the Leader wants to use them for the motorcade. It is likely that the police are not even fully informed about the Leader's itinerary, so they close a few extra boulevards and highway sections just in case.

Traian Băsescu, Joe Biden, Dimitry Medvedev, Hillary Clinton, among others. And today, Putin.

We know they are coming. We change all of our plans for that day. We cancel and postpone appointments. We park our cars for the day (or we should). And we get ready for their visits like a severe weather warning. Those of us who insist on trying to drive around town may be blocked for hours, waiting for the diplomatic high pressure front to subside. Sometimes we are not even allowed to WALK in certain places.

It must be a satisfaction for a world leader to visit the White City on the Danube.

Do Not Pass Go

"If you will excuse me, I REALLY have to hurry."

There was a small crowd gathered in front of the Serbian parliament this afternoon and I had to elbow and head-butt my way through the few but stalwart people blocking my path.

"There is not much time," I protested. "I have to get them to look at my DRAFT CONSTITUTION!"

Silence fell. Suddenly I was the cynosure of all eyes. "Constitution," the word of the day, cut through the opposition like a hot knife through kajmak. Hands suddenly appeared out of nowhere, all reaching to grab the fresh draft of the constitution from under my white knuckles. Inside the parliament building, the powers that be were wrangling and bickering over the watered-down-something-for-everyone-but-nothing-for-Toma draft that appeared on the verge of being agreed. The advent of a possible alternative raised hopes and eyebrows across the windswept square.

When it became apparent that neither I nor the crowd were about to give ground, a small voice was heard from the rear of the throng. "What does it say?" inquired the voice.

My moment having arrived, I opened the brown envelope and unwrapped the rectangular box which I had been guarding so carefully.

"My proposal," I orated, "is a simple one. This constitution was already been written many years ago and is still used all around the world. This draft brings order to chaos."

I knelt and placed the rectangular box on the ground before me. The circle of onlookers closed in tight. I removed the lid of the box and extracted a cardboard square, folded in half and opened it. I removed a small metal race-car, top hat, thimble, dog, and a flatiron, purse, lantern, and shoe. Finally, from the bottom of the box I removed a document with large bold faced letters bearing an unmistakable inscription:

The Rules of Monopoly

I stood up straight again and was preparing to read (a few of the onlookers had dived in to scoop up a few handfuls of play money). Clearing my throat, I looked around and saw, to my surprise, that the crowd had listlessly turned away and was heading back to the parliament building entrance.

"Hang on!" I cried. "Will no one listen to my idea? Why shouldn't the rules of this game apply to the country? Are we not all being bought and sold every day by a handful of extremely rich players? Are not the properties of the country being traded, merged, and bankrupted by a group of nine or ten people?"

The small voice, which had been heard before, was the only one remaining. It belonged to a little boy who picked up the metal dog and was now making assorted barking sounds. His father, in a dark tuxedo, white moustache, and shining top hat approached me and handed me his card. Taking the boy by the hand and turning away to join the others, he uttered only four words to me in answer to the sudden disinterest shown by the heretofore excited spectators.

"Been there," he sighed. "Done that."

Sticky Carrots

Reading the news about Serbia's chances of renewing talks with the EU, I came across a line from the chief Government Talking Head (or Head of Talking, as you like) which baffled me:

"It's a pity that EU talks won't be continued at this time, since that would motivate us to finalize the Hague cooperation as soon as possible," Đurić told the press. (B92, October 15)

Now, it is just possible that I am a little old fashioned about interpreting texts. This I freely admit. But somehow I remember reading that the EU talks had STOPPED in order to motivate the government to cooperate with The Hague…

This back-to-frontism and logical table-turning may explain why the G17Plus G-Men have quit their jobs while remaining steadfastly in office. It may also tell why the new draft constitution zipped through parliament in 6.7 seconds after six years of wrangling and waiting around.

In fact, now that I think about it – this explains EVERYTHING! The heart of the heart of the matter is that when it comes to statements from the government, one-plus-one does not necessarily have to equal two. Or even three. In this cosmic epiphanic moment, I realized that one-plus-one equals:

a) two small tomatoes on a chair somewhere outside Denver, Colorado;

b) an anomalous blip on a radar screen which was probably a weather balloon;

c) 17 cornish hens, roasted;

d) Something else entirely;

e) All of the above.

When you look at it in this way, it is obvious that the carrot-and-stick approach to dealing with the Future Former Serbian Government is really inappropriate and is to be avoided.

Someone out there is certainly going to eat the stick.

Low Stakes Game

Did you notice how they no longer hold our attention?

Elections in Serbia used to be raucous and joyous popular battles. And when I say used to be, I mean last time we had them. The Fate of the Nation was at stake. The choices we made at the polls would determine our Destiny. Our Place in the Universe depended SO MUCH on who we chose. Naturally, the rhetorical warfare of invective and slander was part of the game. OUR GUY was better by far, but, in order to see that, we had to show and be shown how the OTHER GUYS were Evil and Pernicious and even a little Smelly.

Hearing news from the political front today is, on the contrary, annoying and grating, like fingernails on the national chalkboard. Today we roll our eyes when we listen to the whining of the splintered democratic party leaders. It does not seem to matter as much which of the babies in this daycare center is crying the loudest, which ones will not share their toys, which ones want more milk, and which ones just have full diapers.

Few believe any longer that Voja, Boris, Božidar, Velja, Čeda, or Mladjan will put more food on the table, raise the standard of living, restore national prestige, make sense of the tax system, foil the oligarchs, lower inflation, raise salaries, revitalize industry, or reorganize the public sector. We trust them mostly to rename the streets of Belgrade and raise fines for not wearing seatbelts.

The specter of a Radical government, once a force that unified the democratic voters by Fear of the Alternative, has grown faded and tattered as we have watched them take the big numbers in every post-2000 election but only half-heartedly fight to wrest the reigns of power from the squabbling heirs of DOS. Somehow we have the feeling that they will be sitting on the opposition benches again this time, watching a weak and infantile minority or a just-barely-majority, rife with internal discord over coalition compromises, squeak by and inflict the same nongovernance of the country's affairs on the people.

We are complacent. They are loud but also complacent. We will NOT get the government we deserve, but whatcha gonna do?

If this sounds cynical and jaded, there is a very specific reason for it. It is because this IS cynical and jaded. It just seems to me, in my position of disenfranchised foreigner (i.e., without a vote) who has CHOSEN to live here and therefore opted to take whatever comes along in terms of a government, that the stakes have never been lower. The future government of Serbia cannot – no matter who does it – create a Serbian utopia just because it sits in the big chairs. So far, the battle seems to be more about chairs than the game that is actually on the table. My jaded and cynical view tells me that once the chairs have been divvied out, the game on the table will be played according to the same seat-of-your-pants strategies that we have come to expect of our standard players.

On January 22, when we wake up in the morning, we will discover who we have chosen in the papers. We will tell ourselves that we KNEW it all along. And 40 days later, we will have our brand new government which looks eerily a lot like the old one.

Whatcha gonna do?

UnREAL
POLITIK

DAY IN THE LIFE

DAY IN THE LIFE

Another glorious day in Belgrade! Another day in which your expectations of normal life may be summarily tipped into the trash and you may go forth, knowing full well that nothing usual will happen on this day.

The trick is to look casual when the dog stew is served.

In Belgrade, and perhaps even in other places on this planet, stuff happens every day.

Most of it is visible and can be noted. The chicken, for example, who gets up early. The obsessive person who, for example, writes blogs.

This section is really just a hodgepodge of different, random, and mostly irrelevant discourse which affords the intrepid reader a look into my cavernous mind. It is not a pretty sight – be forewarned.

If, on the other hand, you have wondered about the similarities between the Klingon and Serbian languages, as most of us have often done, this is the place for you. What to do when the world ends (or if not the world, just the current year) is another imponderable. We shout hurrah at midnight, but THEN what?

Break a few resolutions?

Too Hip, Gotta Go

I just found out I am too old to be a hipster. I am just old-fashioned. If I were under 30, then old-fashioned would qualify as hipster. Thus spake the Urban Dictionary.

The hipster has become ubiquitous. They sport my old clothes. They wear my old glasses. They listen to music which either predates me or hasn't yet been invented. In fact, every time that I sorted through my old things and gave them away, I was helping to forge the Hipster.

It is a great responsibility.

The word Hipster seems to derivate directly from Hippie. Hippies in the 1960s and 70s had a sort of agenda: rejection of traditional values, anti-war, free love, freeing themselves from the death-grip of societal restrictions. As a counterculture, they were knocked for a loop one fine morning when they woke to see that (suddenly) they had won. Hippy culture stopped being rejected and was co-opted by the very society that had been the oppressor. Why? Because the hippies grew up and *became* it.

My parents' generation (and arguably my parents themselves) were genuine hippies.

The house where we lived from 1972-1978 was painted in kaleidoscopic polychromes in the middle of a staunchly conservative Iowa town. They preferred browns, grays, and whites. I remember old farmers chiding my dad for his wild-man beard at a local diner. We wore homemade and second-hand clothes. We ate alfalfa and granola and carob instead of chocolate.

Although I was still a kid, hippie-ness had begun already to transform from rebellion into cool. We all had bell-bottoms. We wore peace signs around our necks. We had aviator sunglasses. We got a little mixed up between being a 70s dude and being a 50s Fonzie, but the course was pretty much steady through the decade.

In the 80s, of course, the winds changed and gradually drifted from the coolness of the post-hippie into the hard-edged Gordon Gekko model of trendy. In the meantime, the intergenerational preppies and yuppies invaded and retreated.

Fast forward (another hipster-friendly term since my old cassette recorder belongs to them now) to yesterday afternoon at about 3:30, and we now have hipsters everywhere. This is not plain old retro style – they seem to want to become a class of humanity. The main difference I see between the hippies and the hipsters lies in the intention. Hippies rejected the outward appearance or external influence on them. Hipsters, on the other hand, are all about the look.

If you examine them carefully, you will detect an attention to detail that is highly developed. Not all glasses frames are accepted: they should be large, black, and Walter Cronkite-like. The colors are not hippie psychedelic but relatively subdued, if mixed eccentrically.

The hipster is proud of being different from the masses crowding his *Zeitgeist*. He does not notice that the masses around him aspire to being hipsters too. It's just too hip not to be. Jerry Seinfeld, in his "Comedians in Cars Getting Coffee", observed the endemic irony of these dare-to-be-differenters. "If they were really hipsters," he said, "how could there be so many of them?"

This is not a counter-culture. This is what we have become. Future historians will look on to this decade and wonder if this was the pivotal point where the human race just ran out of ideas.

In the home, the hipster likes "shabby chic". To a hipster generation generator such as I, this means that all of the old, poorly painted furniture which we threw out of French farmhouses has now become a Recognized Style. The term shabby chic was invented by a writer for the *World of Interiors* in the 80s but is only now coming into its own. The definition is "a form of interior design where furniture and furnishings are either chosen for their appearance of age and signs of wear and tear or where new items are distressed to achieve the appearance of an antique." The new old is new – but old.

But new. Whatever.

One day, gazing into the future, when I am a guru sitting high atop a mountain in Tibet, young pilgrim hipsters will come to ask the one question which will turn their lives around and give them meaning:

"How did you dress in 1984?"

Arranged to Save the World

The universe is out of whack. We know it.

And it is all out of our control. Earthquakes quake. Weather squalls. Clouds cumulate. What can anyone do to combat this? Human fallibility on the other hand creates a whole new set of wrong-angle situations – trains derail, airplanes get lost over Malaysia, fanatics get elected to positions of power, armies roll in, and someone wears a red shirt with yellow striped pants.

True story. I have seen that guy.

The question, therefore, is not why all this happens or what we can do (no reason and nothing), but why we ALL do not have obsessive compulsive disorder (OCD) or Compulsive Disorder Obsessive (arranged alphabetically).

People make fun of us. They say we are sick. They say we are dysfunctional. But the universe is out of whack, and the only thing we can do is set to rights the things over which we have at least a modicum of control.

So we go about straightening pictures, adjusting refrigerator magnets into symmetrical patterns, closing doors, turning off lights, and checking to see if we closed the doors and turned off the lights. Twice. When the universe is out of whack, what else can be done?

By creating order, we are acting against the Prime Mover who is (let's face it) sloppy in his/her/its work. The Prime Mover likes the big picture. He likes to try out 'what if' scenarios. He is infinitely curious about stuff. What if that mountain suddenly crumbled? What if those six boats hit each other in open water? What if people were given the choice of their leaders?

Humans are particularly interesting to the Prime Mover, because they will do things that defy explanation – and yet they will explain. One could argue that the Prime Mover made them that way. But he also peppered the world with the OCD in order to try to make it right. To bring order to chaos.

We are the last bastions of asserting control over the uncontrollable. We do not believe in chaos theory. We see patterns, and we strive to restore them.

I believe that the Prime Mover believes he is "artistic". He feels that it is not important to conform to rules or follow any guidelines. He wants to be free to express himself. He colors outside the lines. He thinks outside the box. He pushes the envelope. The OCD do not argue with that, but we counter with a different approach. Give him differently drawn lines for coloring. Bigger boxes. More flexible envelopes.

The real problem which we OCDians face is that, at times, the effort to fight the askew can overwhelm us, leading us to forego our own lives in the struggle to make the universe adhere to its own pattern. This is the real menace – not OCD per se, but OOCD.

Obsessive Obsessive Compulsive Disorder.

While the universe remains out of whack, OCDians must find a (perfectly symmetrical) balance between maintaining order on a macro level (my neighbor's house), on a micro level (my desk), and at the same time find a way to lead a normal life. This is by no means easy. But if we do not, the mass of people will discount our efforts at perpendicularity, orthogonal rectitude, and dendroid unicoherency as the product of an unwell mind.

We straighten pictures from a sense of duty. We are massively misunderstood creatures, we OCDians. We work to make YOUR world a better more orderly place. If the Prime Mover is an artist who flaunts the rules, doesn't that imply that there ARE rules? If we break with convention, we need conventions. And who best to safeguard the rules and conventions but us?

We cannot rewhack the universe. But we can manage our corner of it.

Reverse Backsliding

Time for a change. Again.

At the moment of the transition from one year into the next one, I am always confronted by a Troubling Paradox. The Christmas and New Year's (or New Year's and Christmas in Orthodox juxtaposition) holidays always urge me to Observe Tradition and Incite Revolution. The Tradition comes for me at Christmas, wherein I am compelled to do all the same things I have done all my life. And Revolution comes at 23:59 on December 31 when I feel compelled to change all those things I have always done.

I hate paradoxes. They give me a headache.

To make matters worse, the Troubling Paradox is coupled with a Singular Irony. The Singular Irony is that observing the traditions is a pain in the hindquarters, and the big life changes usually last about seven seconds before the backslide.

All these capitalized words also give me a headache.

The Christmas traditions which I observe are quite minimal. The tree should go up in the second week of December and come down on or around Twelfth Night (January 5th). The tradition also embraces a Christmas Eve dinner (without a set menu, but involving some elaborate cooking) and Christmas breakfast the next morning consisting of pancakes, eggs, and sausages. The breakfast proceeds the opening of presents followed by a day of doing little else than assembling toys and hanging around.

And that is it. The pain in the hindquarters comes in the planning, getting ready, making menus, shopping, wrapping, and making time to do it all. Even if we have all year to get ready for it, Christmas always seems to sneak up on me – as much as a fixed date on a calendar can be sneaky.

Then the first rumblings of the revolution start to be heard. Distant drums in the background. New Year's Day is only a week away and the usual list of resolutions beckons. On my usual list we have Quit Smoking, Quit Eating Junk, Lose Weight, Read More Books, and Watch Less TV. Added to this in recent years: Stop-Checking-Facebook-Every-10-Seconds.

Facebook seriously takes away from my TV time....

Every year I REALLY believe in these resolutions, but each year (traditionally) most of them are forgotten by the time I wake up on January 1 with any of a wide variety of headaches. And any resolutions which survive will succumb to the backslide within a week at the most.

In addition to the Singular Irony in which I would like to revolutionize instead of keeping tradition and keep my bad habits instead of revolting against them, there is the Supplementary Irony in which I *know* very well all this but carry on regardless.

Can you start to feel the headache with me?

So far there is no evidence that any of these traditions and paradoxes and ironies will do anything different from any other year. But this year I have run head on into the stark and unsettling realization that I do not have to conform to all this conditioning. I see what I do – I see what would be better – and I do what is not. What is wrong with this picture?

The reality is that all the tradition is just another way of justifying habits. It is easier, in a way, to keep traditions because they relieve me of any decision-making. "Because-that-is-what-we-do" has become an acceptable answer. If "what we do" means "what I have always done," then it can be changed. And it does not have to be a revolution. Or a resolution. Or a paradox.

THEREFORE (and I know we took a long time to come to the THEREFORE, but here it comes now), instead of committing to change things and then backsliding, I shall perform the Reverse Backslide. Next year will not be as much about making new traditions and new resolutions and then backsliding, I will proceed directly to the backslide, thereby accomplishing everything in one deft bit of mental acrobatics.

I will fool myself into fooling myself that I plan to do things differently. And then do the opposite.

For those of you to whom this makes no sense, I assure you that it is perfect nonsense. Don't rush for the paracetamol yet. The Reverse Backslide means ironing out the Troubling Paradox, shaking out the Singular Irony, and washing out the Supplementary Irony. THAT will be my non-resolution.

And I fully intend to break it. And then ignore my intentions.

A Quiet War

Shhh…. Belgrade has gone to sleep.

There was a time, though, when the White City on the Danube woke up at midnight. It was perfectly normal for people to make arrangements to meet at and around midnight when the movable feast of clubbing and cafes and bars and even restaurants would bestir itself, singing and playing into the wee small hours of the morning.

Or at least so they tell me.

They have to tell me these things because I am far more likely to be recruited by the group of grumpy old (and young apparently) guys calling themselves "*Beogradani protiv noćne buke.*" They are currently proselytizing around town and have even lobbied the Powers That Be into the early closings of clubs and bars and other noise factories which used to work throughout the white nights of the White City.

Why me? I am guilty of liking to sleep at night. I have grumbled about midnight hooting in the street. Given a wide array of choice, I would not be likely to choose hearing turbo-ethno-neo-stupid music blaring into my window far above the decimal limit for humans when I am trying to sleep.

As an American living here for ten years, the (former) legendary nightlife of Belgrade has always been the stuff of stories that foreigners ask me when arriving here. They want to know if it is true. For my own reasons, I have never really experienced these nocturnal habits so I tell them all that I know: "that's what they say."

But the move to close down the merry-makers cuts in two ways. The first is to appease the Middle Aged Lynch Mob, and the second is (of course) to rake in a few extra dinars. Most bars and restaurants have been used to keeping the music playing and wine pouring into the night, until the last stragglers actually straggle out. In reality, most of them are probably licensed only until midnight. After midnight, you need to apply for special permission to be open. This, clearly, ka-chings in the municipal coffers.

The city is now enforcing the noise laws and the closing hours with surprising strictness – in the hopes, I believe, of forcing establishments to cough up for the extensions to their licenses. But the opposite seems to have happened. Walking around Belgrade at around ten in the evening, the sidewalks are already being rolled up and stowed away. Places that can and should be open until eleven or twelve will now close even earlier – the night owls have flown, knowing that the music will stop at 23.00 and the wine at midnight.

As a result, downtown Belgrade at night has become a desert, inhabited only by polystyrene cows and wandering lost souls wondering where everyone went. The *Beograđani protiv noćne buke* watch from their laced windows with smug smiles as Belgrade transmogrifies into Geneva.

And they turn to me and nod knowingly, looking for my complicity in the plot to put a damper on the city. But I cannot. I think one might be reminded of at least one irritating fact when sitting before the Quiet Committee.

To wit: Belgrade is a city. Clarification: Belgrade is NOT a country town of 26 people, two (real) cows, and a smattering of random chickens. In this condensed mass of two million odd people, we have to admit to ourselves that there WILL BE a little noise.

And by the way, I have lived near farms before. These animals make the worst noises at the earliest hours. Please sign my petition against Night Nature.

The Chickens

With the holidays finished, it is time to start getting up early again. I tell people that I work better in the morning. And while I have been sticking to that story since the late 50s, I wonder if it is very true anymore.

"Getting up with the chickens" is often how it is called – this habit of rising at dawn. But I have no empirical proof that chickens do get up THAT early (I have never felt compelled to make a study of it) or that they make effective use of their time, having woken up with… well… *themselves*. Still the name sticks.

Chickens are a strange, silly, and tragic breed of bird.

I know people who keep chickens right here in Belgrade, in their homes. Their chickens and adherent eggs are touted as being of superior quality, otherwise known as "*domaći*." Domestic eggs and chickens MUST be better even if they are raised in dark cellars and basements rather than on industrial farms.

But I digress. Chickens don't fly, they don't hunt. What, then, are they doing getting up so ridiculously early in the morning? Is it only for the benefit of our being able to think there is another poor creature that has to greet the rising sun as do we when we get up for work?

When the alarm goes off and we groan, does it give us a wry smile of *Schadenfreude* to think that, out there, on some farm, far away, the Chickens are already up and moving about?

Chickens don't even need coffee.

These days I would like to get up with those annoying chickens again. Active and Productive do not engage much before 9 anymore, but when I allow myself to sleep until 9, 10, or 11, I end up feeling guilty – as though I have lost the day, slept through it.

And inexorably my mind returns to the chickens. They are up early, yes, but they are doing little else than scurrying around and making a great deal of noise. They have no email to answer, no pitch proposals to create, no columns or blogs to write. Their early-rising is senseless and futile. Do I really need to emulate this behavior? Am I really unable to use my 16 or 17 hours of consciousness effectively if they begin mid-morning?

The answer is quite simple. I shall rise with and/or before these flightless fowl in order to assert my Humanity. Getting up and doing things while still sleepy, I defy my own nature and stick a finger in the eye of the Designer. But do I truly need to prove to anyone that I am somehow better than a chicken?

[AUTHOR'S NOTE: These are the thoughts which occur between the first alarm and the hitting of snooze button. Wake me later and we can discuss.]

Original Content

I do what I do because I have always done it.

There are two reasons for this. The first is that, having done what I do over a considerable time, I have become adept at it. But another reason is that it is more acceptable from a societal point of view to establish continuity and therefore predictability in my persona. People know me in that I do the things that I do because I have always done them.

We need people to be as we expect them to be. It helps us categorize and manage the floods of humanity which is otherwise doing more or less the same things we do. We eat, we sleep, we reproduce. Repeat. But if we KNOW that some guy always eats with his left hand even if he is right-handed, we can pin him to that particular exhibit and move on. We need no further contemplate him as a person because his persona has distinguished attributes.

In my case, I have long done things slightly differently from my peers and fellows – not enough to be labeled as crazy, but perhaps just enough to gain the status of eccentric (i.e., off-center). While everyone else wears ties, I have Nehru collars. When people nod and agree, I dispute. When everyone else disputes, I nod and agree. Over time, I have come to understand that this does not happen out of a need to be different, but rather as a reaction to what appears to me to be rampant and unthinking conformity.

We all like to be the same, to some extent. But do we choose it or are we compelled to try to be the same?

If tomorrow I begin to do things as NEVER I have done them before, does it make a statement about my previous actions? It would if you considered other peoples' boxes as a True Home. When I start to act outside the box which I have been assigned, the mass of humanity which may know me will begin to reclassify and open a new box for me. In other words, my persona is infinitely the persona of the moment.

And people HATE to reclassify…

This means that, if I reclassify someone I know into a new and previously unknown category, I must accept the possibility of reclassifying or changing myself. If everything remains the same, then so do I. If things can change, then so can I. This is terrifying.

The notion of Original Content, to me, speaks to considered content. The content of one's Life Thus Far, in other words, need not be the content of one's total life. Tomorrow could bring change (or the next minute) or not. And if change is inevitable, why do we oppose it so vehemently if not because – like the others who box us – we box ourselves as well. We have a residual self-image which is how we view ourselves and our place in the universe. There is an erroneous notion that, if I choose to reconsider my place in the universe, that my Life Thus Far was somehow wrong.

The reality however is different. The reality is that change is constant, and the decision to buck against change and be the same as we perceive ourselves and as others perceive us is a *conscious* decision. We are stuck in an endless chain of decision-making which leads us to do and be and act and speak exactly as we did yesterday so that we continue to know ourselves.

If this is done with consideration and thought, then perhaps it is original. But I suspect that it is not, in most cases. I suspect that it is a product of habit and conditioning. As such, the habits can be broken and the conditioning thrown aside.

QUESTION: Will today be different?

No Going Back Now

No matter what we do, the next step is always forward.

It is a fact of our linear time-space continuum that the life in the world is a one way street. 2011 cannot be followed by 2010 (nor by 1526 as far as that goes) or anything other than 2012. Tonight we celebrate that passage in our odd and somewhat superfluous tradition marking the passage of time. Even as I write this, we could be celebrating the passage of 11.59 into 12.00…

Happy New Afternoon, everyone! Should auld acquaintance et cetera et cetera!

There will be chronicles of the past year playing across televisions and YouTube channels for most of the day and even into tomorrow and the next week, outtakes and clips where we look back and review our most recent history, getting ready all the while for the next year.

Some of us would like to carry on into 2012 with the same tempo and leitmotif as has been playing until now. Others of us would wish that 2012 could be started *tabula rasa* and that we really could forget the auld acquaintance of the outgoing year and start afresh. Sadly, to do such a thing would hardly be feasible. Wipe out the collective history of the species and reboot?

Our linear progression through the human construct of time allows neither "back" nor a "clear cache" option (he quipped, extending the metaphor a little too far). Whatever has happened in the now waning 2011 is set down in evidence while the unwritten events of the waxing 2012 will be tinged and tainted and colored by them.

The only way we can affect the past now is in its interpretation. Everything that happened happened. But what the individual and collective consciousness can do now is spin past events in their burden of meaning and their significance. We are able to reorder events in order of importance or magnitude and assign new meanings which will, in turn, allow us to plan for 2012. We can say to ourselves that this year we will do THIS better or

THAT differently or THE OTHER THING in a manner more conducive to a fortuitous outcome.

In the end, we are stuck with our histories but not our futures.

Herein is the paradoxical paradigm of the New Year's celebrations. Life, as John Lennon famously stated, is what happens when you are making other plans. So we plan and plot and scheme and outline and forecast and look ahead and try to guess what we will do in the coming year, but we will finally do what we do regardless of plans. Sometimes, in retrospect, we will see that reality and projections match up. But mostly all we do is take each new step forward – our planning only gives us the illusion that our next step will not be into a mud puddle.

If all this seems a little gloomy and existentialist, it is not. Ask me if I would recast and reorder and change things about this outgoing year and I will tell you that I would not. This is not because everything went swimmingly, all being for the best in the best of all possible worlds. In fact this year was a bit of swine for me in many ways. Still, the inexpungeable record of 2011 can do no other than shape the as yet untold story of 2012.

And I cling to the hope that I might have learned something from it.

Happy New Year

Getting Around

Let it be said, from the very beginning, that I have the worst sense of direction in the history of Human Disorientation. Even after eight years living here, I have been known to get lost in Belgrade, occasionally in my own neighborhood, and, at the very worst, in large supermarkets.

Be that as it may, would it kill us to put up a few street signs?

There are cities which do NOT allow you to get lost. Each corner is sign-posted with the name of the street and the directions you need to go – train station, city center, zoo, airport, Museum of Natural History, or corner shop where you buy city maps. Belgrade is not such a city however. And Serbia, by and large, is not such a country.

It would seem that there is a premium here on knowing your way around by instinct. As a right of initiation, the new arrival to the White City on the Danube must gain his or her own orientation, unaided by the City of Belgrade.

And by the way, it took me several years to know which was the Danube and which was the Sava...

Entries and exits to the highways are also a great mystery to me. Traveling south towards Niš, I have taken almost every exit to get to Smederevo (I think there are four) before stumbling upon the right one. Each is intrepidly marked "Smederevo" and the driver is forced to intuit the correct one for his purposes. Somehow, whenever I tell anyone about my problems in knowing which way to go, they are always laughing.

"How do I get to the center of Smederevo?"

"Take the Smederevo exit."

"Which ONE?"

"The one for the center, of course!"

In the city it is not better. Belgrade city streets often have more than one name and people tend to use whichever one they remember as part of their cultural inheritance. Older people will tell you to go down Lole Ribara, Bulevar AVNOJ-a, Bulevar 29. Novembra, Narodnog Fronta and Bulevar Mira (which would be a strange itinerary, but nevertheless…) and the newbie would struggle to find these ghost streets. Ironically, four of those name changes happened during my tenure here in Belgrade and I STILL can make mistakes about them.

The foreigner in Belgrade, therefore, needs to track along through the city on foot, deciphering the Cyrillic names of streets and constructing a map in his head. Problematically, if your head is constructed like mine, you will retain the topographic survey for approximately 26 minutes and then get lost again around the next blind corner.

I admit to my bad sense of direction, although I am not sure if I have made such a full confession of it until now. Men, in fact, seldom admit to this. We never ask directions. We would prefer to be horribly lost than to admit defeat and roll down the window. But after driving up and down Poenkareova six or seven times looking for the turn off to Tempo (which is indicated 1500 meters away without arrows), I throw up my arms and beg passersby to show me the way.

If ever a project comes up to install more signage in Belgrade and around the country, I will be among the first to sign up to help. You can find me easily, I am the one driving round and round Slavija.

Speak Warriors!

T'lhIngan maH! Kai kassai!

In my continuing quest to learn the Serbian language (a quest which is often interrupted and curtailed by intervening events, obligations, and Tuesdays), I have come to realize that I have overlooked an essential part of learning this language that has nothing to do with my six-word vocabulary, my mastery of one tense and one grammatical case, or my inability to deal with multiple declensions.

Attitude.

If you have never heard of Star Trek, the Klingon Empire, or Kahless the Unforgettable, you may want to open a new tab and do some research before continuing. The fact is that, as a spoken language, Serbian must be enunciated and bellowed out like Klingon. Sentences are marked by exclamation marks. Words declaratively expressed in CAPITAL LETTERS!

The Klingon does not brook the mealy-mouthed, the overly polite, the sycophantic, or the obsequious. In fact, the language may not even contain equivalents to these words.

Imagine, if you will, the scene in the restaurant. The room is crowded and only one or two waiters hover among the tables. You (meaning *me*, the Anglo-Saxon) are thirsty. You raise your hand tentatively, attracting exactly NO attention. The waiters dive and swoop around you without knowing you are there. You then assert yourself with a timid, "Excuse me?"

Nothing.

After about fifteen minutes of this pantomime, he finally happens to be near you and you state your request: "Excuse me, but if you would not mind, if you happen to be passing by the kitchen and if it is not any trouble, I would appreciate a glass of water, please. When you get around to it, next time you are near the table. Thank you."

Before you have completed your request, however, the waiter has completely lost interest and has flitted off to another, more decisive table. Without knowing, you have committed the un-forgiveable offense of being inoffensive. It is not that that wait-er actually wants you to be rude; it is just that he understands the rude and the preemptory much better. The flurry of Nice-ness which you have spread into the air between yourself and the waiter only gets in his eyes, and he does not know what you want until you have littered the order with 36 unnecessary words. Consequently, and having no time to work it out, he re-moves himself.

Imagine the same scene, however, sung in a different key. You are thirsty. You declare yourself. You cry out "DEČKO!" This is already upsetting your Anglo Saxon sensibilities as you are refer-ring to man who may be more than one decade your senior as "boy." Try ŠEFE! (chief) instead.

"Water!"

"*More blood wine!*" cries the Klingon warrior. And he slams his fist upon the table, breaking out in a laugh which fills the en-tire room. The waiter will arrive instantly. He will smile with you, he will nod, and within an instant drop off a glass of wa-ter on the table. This exchange consisted of two words, an op-tional gesture, and lasted about three minutes. And no one was put out or offended. The mealy-mouthed and polite Anglo-Sax-on way required several full paragraphs (with footnotes and dis-claimers), nearly 20 minutes, and in the end, a bitter taste in your mouth and an annoyed waiter (who may never return to your table again).

It is in the attitude. It is the assertive natural tone of the lan-guage. Speak loudly Warriors!

Speak clearly and proudly! Use fewer words! It is the way! It is OUR way!

I would only ask, if it is not a problem, and only if you think of it at the time, NOT to mention where you heard all this if you attempt a practical application. My *bat'leth* is in the shop being sharpened this week.

Planet Earth: Signing Off

So this is goodbye.

Chances are that the world will have ended by the time I finish this sentence. No? Ok, I can probably get a few more paragraphs in before the cataclysm and what St. Matthew calls the time of "great tribulation" (clearly a biblical Star Trek reference, indicating how well he could see the future).

The big question must be HOW the world is going to be ended. Millions of years in the making, surely the denouement will have to be something spectacular. No mere separation of the sheep from the goats, the Book of Revelations promises us a 3D sound-and-light extravaganza that will (quite literally) blow our minds.

And then, as the world will be at an end after the show, no need to remember where we parked.

[*Checks at the window; notes continued existence of the world; pours a drink*].

It is deeply gratifying to me that you are sending these last few moments before the destruction of civilization and all of its delights and devastations with me. It does put a bit of added pressure on me to ensure that the last words you are reading will be of SIGNIFICANCE and might even be of some use in the Hereafter.

[*Nothing yet?*]

Sadly, as TS Eliot would have it, the world will probably end with more of whimper than a bang. Much in the way Osama bin Laden was dealt with – wham, bam, thank you ma'am, where's the body? We will receive the new of our destruction in real time thus making it far less dramatic than the End of the World deserves. Real time always disappoints as the action is always far more quickly dispatched than the narrative version could make it. Suddenly the lights will snap off. We will curse and blame the storm (rather a nice meteorological touch for E. of the W.), and then suddenly it will be:

"Damn!"

"What?"

"The world has ended."

"It's probably just a fuse…"

Assuming the worst, however, we should probably have all out Monday morning affairs in order nevertheless. The excuse about the world NOT ending when it should have will probably not fly. No one will take pity on our lost souls if we try to use that old chestnut. Best rely on Blaise Pascal's old standby for believing in God – if you believe and it turns out he does not exist, what's the harm? But the contrary could get you into a spot of bother on Judgment Day (i.e., today).

[Still got a world out there…]

Just a moment ago, I spoke with a very good friend in Singapore who is already firmly into tomorrow time-zone wise. Talking to her was like talking to the future. And in the future, she exists, therefore… et cetera.

But just in case this is goodbye, thanks for the memories.

Planet Earth: signing off.

Reasons Not to Speak Serbian:
An Annotated List

Recently I find myself telling people how long I have been here. It is also a recent phenomenon that people begin to compliment my Serbian. I always say thank you. But I know the truth…

The ugly truth is that I have been here for nearly a decade and communicate here like a Balinese coconut-picker landed suddenly in the middle of a Parisian dinner party. In the court of Louis XVI.

Of a Tuesday afternoon.

The following are reasons, rationalizations, justifications, apologies, and excuses and are only part of a whole complex system which seems not to allow me (see how I shift the blame away from myself?) to perfect my imperfect Serbian language "skills".

Reason Number 61.   EVERYONE SPEAKS ENGLISH TO ME

While this seems like a cheap and or lame excuse, it is true that every time I try to put three words together in Serbian someone will ask me in crystal clear Queen's English if I am going to be sick. Such do I sound, I suppose, to the lay-listener.

Reason Number 538.   I CANNOT REMEMBER THE WORDS

Without sending myself an undue amount of flowers, I already speak four languages – but they all somewhat resemble each other. This means that an Italian word can be floated into French with an appropriate accent and, while still being wrong, can pass as comprehensible. But none of these words sound ANYTHING like Serbian.

I have stood innumerable times in open-mouthed silence before an interlocutor trying to give birth to the Right Word or an approximation thereof or something that might mean something similar or even something that is completely different just to fill the silence. Mouth open, eyes apoplectic, brow perspiring, and no sounds coming out.

The words. I cannot remember the words. Otherwise I speak fluently.

Reason Number 707. THE STRATEGIC ADVANTAGE IN "NOT" SPEAKING

Question: is it a real advantage to be able to understand when the person in front of you is insulting you, thinking all the while that you do not understand? In order to maintain the pretense, I cannot respond either in kind or even in gesture or facial expression. One therefore adopts as bland a visage as possible, making oneself exponentially more ridiculous.

Traffic cops and other officials seem to see through this position however. And anyway they tend to speak English in the alternative. And when they do speak English, the amount of the "fine" tends to increase in proportion to the GDP of the United States.

So this is no real advantage.

Reason Number 3,173. THE TREACHERY OF HALF--UNDERSTANDING

This is pernicious. When, in the middle of a flowing conversation which has ebbed and risen and gone around many bends, I will suddenly understand something which was said about 22 minutes previously. But as the Wernicke's area of my temporal lobe has been busily processing the reception of the language up until now, I did not perceive the passage of those 22 minutes.

When I then blurt out my response, 22 minutes and several conversations too late, I am treated to a round of uncomprehending looks, and, normally, manage to kill the conversation altogether. The looks continue until I have slid underneath my chair and hidden my head completely.

*****

These are only four entries out of the unabridged 36 volume set on the Reasons Not to Speak Serbian. I note them here just in case, as has happened to me on rare occasions, people may wish to address language to me. It will help in the interpretation of the cold sweats, the trembling, and the general agitation which is produced as a result under such interrogation as *"Gde si?"*

Uh….ummm…ahh…. Forget it.

Like Riding a Bike

The expression, "it's like riding a bike" generally means it is something easy and something you do not forget. Whoever said this probably forgot.

The following started out as a letter to a good friend who gave me his mountain bike before absconding to the jungles of South America, but in the meantime has taken on wider significance for me.

Dear Cameron,

The day started out on an optimistic note – sun shining over a generally cold fall morning, perfect weather to take out the bike and ride. This was my morning thought over coffee and cigarettes (training supplements of choice to the serious cyclist).

I knew things were headed downhill (actually uphill would be more accurate) when, after kitting myself out in heretofore unused biking clothes, I found that the tires were both deflated. You conferred the bike on me already several months ago, but I have not used it more than once. It required a small investment in a lock and somehow I did not get around to getting one until now. The reason for this is simple: ONCE I BUY THE LOCK I HAVE NO MORE EXCUSES NOT TO RIDE.

So I took out the little pump I bought from you and set to pumping. After about 30 minutes, I realized I was doing something horribly wrong. I was sweating profusely and the tires had lost even more air. This was a decisive moment. At this stage I stupidly decided that this bike will not defeat me, and I carried downstairs and onto the street to look for a gas station with a compressor.

An unexpected benefit of this was the discovery of my neighborhood.

I found that my neighborhood in Palilula *(I am sorry I just like to say this name: Palilula. It sounds like a Baptist minister who had been sipping the communion wine. "Praise the Lord, sing* pallilujah!*)* has no fewer than five gas stations. Each of them has an air compressor, but not one was in working order. As I arrived at each, I was sent to the next one in a kind of treasure hunt.

When I arrived at Number Five, the guy sent me to a Vulkanizer. He gave me instructions which sounded a little like this: "Mnjadualjalalamnjadualjala Vulkanizer." Maybe I was just tired by then and could not process words anymore. I had been walking the bike around the streets of Pallilujah at this stage for about an hour. I set off along the road to which he pointed and, after about 20 minutes, found a line of Vulkanizers.

SIDE NOTE: I'm fairly sure Vulkanizer is not a real word in English….

Happy to see the busy tire shop, I walked the bike up to a guy who was standing next to an air compressor which seemed to be in good condition. I asked him if someone could help me and he said No. No time. Wrong nozzle. Wrong valve. Busy.

Disgruntled and not believing his excuses, I proceeded to the next three tires shops. In the last of these, I found a guy who was ready, willing, and able. He made quick work of my vexing problem which first beset me two hours and about sixteen kilometers ago. I thanked him profusely.

Now the world suddenly looked different. Suddenly I was enabled to ride this bike. I realized a few things straight away. I no longer knew where I was – having traipsed around aimlessly for so long I was now in an unfamiliar corner of Palilula (if indeed I was still in Palilula at all, or Belgrade for that matter). I also realized that any way back from this place was uphill. And finally, I realized that I had forgotten how to work the gears on the bike (I know you showed me, but the information was just gone).

This all happened, my dear Cameron, yesterday. Today, from the calm perspective of my kitchen table, it all seems like a fable. How I got on the bike and rode up the hill in the hardest gear (and I am not sure if this is 1 or 18). How I rode through the traffic on Belgrade's bigger streets and boulevards, making every driver furious with me, because it was the only way I knew. And how, sweating and palpitating, at the end of my journey which finally took about eight minutes even if it seemed like hours, I parked and locked the bike in front of my gym. For exercise.

In a very few minutes, I will start this two-wheeled odyssey again, although the car keys are sitting next to me, and I feel my hand moving closer to them. And I probably have not yet had enough cigarettes and coffee to enhance the experience yet. But as you told me, it will get easier in time.

I think ten years may just be enough.

"Did you hear....?"

This is going to be tricky.

The thing is about rumors: all you need is the vaguest insinuation of something for it to begin passing along great unseen chains of whispers and embellishments until everyone directly interested and indirectly uninterested – and some people quite frankly exasperated – suddenly knows. It passes into common knowledge. And suddenly, the best rumors are then apotheosized into the greatest of all possible forms of knowledge.

They become the TRUTH.

Belgrade is not such a small city, demographically speaking. But in real terms it is approximately the size of a goldfish bowl. Why I said this is going to be tricky is because the mere *idea* of writing about rumors (even about "rumors" as a plural noun and at all about any *specific* rumor) implies that there is some juicy tidbit lurking in the back of the writer's mind causing him to think about writing about rumors. A hidden truth is implied.

And it is positively *untrue* that I am doing PR for the Queen of England.

Rumors are generally born of speculation. Somewhere in the deep background there is probably some actual fact – a guy stumbles upon some small fraction of information which led him to wonder and guess about its origin, background, and meaning. Then, unable to find any other supporting facts, the guy tells another guy: "I bet that means that...." And the guy who receives this speculation passes it on like this: "I heard that...." And then rumoristic truths are born.

Rumoristic is not a word.

In the time I have been living here, which is rapidly becoming immense, I have heard hundreds of these Truth Rumors. I have been the subject of one or two of (which I am aware) and have probably started a few dozen as well. Unintentionally, of course. All it takes is a bit of idle talk at the water-cooler or a stray thought given voice at a cocktail party and suddenly the rumor takes on a life force which is as vigorous as a garden weed.

Coupled with the fascination people have about spreading rumors all over the world, there is another element which makes rumoring in the White City much more pernicious: the urge to report. Many is the time where I have met someone on the street, or in a shop, or anywhere, and just as I have turned to leave, the person's mobile phone has been activated. He must now report: *"Hey, I just saw Chris. He was wearing something green. He seemed in a hurry."* The reporter sends his report and, at times, this report is reported further along the chain (altered a little as these things happen) until, by the time I arrive back in the office, the report is fed to me as Information.

"I heard you looked green and were in a hurry to throw up…"

Now, let it be said that the reason for this blog is only because I did indeed hear an interesting and patently untrue rumor recently. It is all the more interesting because it seems that it is connected with a person or persons unknown whom I may or may not know and I have understood the details may be products of a lively imagination. Or not.

But I resist the urge to report.

Coming Soon: Dog Stew

Courtesy of Messrs. Wong, Kim, Idibia, and Farmer, the long awaited New Belgrade opening of "Psi" shall be feted this evening. On the menu: Boshintang, or Korean Dog Meat Stew, or Guyouk-geng Minnan, otherwise known as "fragrant meat" of Taiwanese dogs. We await your pleasure, tails wagging.

New Belgrade is soon to join the list, including China, Korea, Nigeria, Indonesia, Japan, Poland, Germany, France, Tahiti, Switzerland, Ghana, Siberia, Alaska, Greenland, and many more countries across the glove who either open and notoriously or clandestinely consume dog meat.

It tastes like chicken, they say.

In Albania they say, it tastes like hedgehog.

The idea for this new restaurant was born only recently. In these interview excerpts from

Mr. Wong and Mr. Farmer, we see a little of the driving force behind it.

WONG: My native Northern Jiangsu is well-known in China for its dog-meat stew flavored with soft-shelled turtle. Here there are plentiful dogs, running wild around New Belgrade. No one takes care of them. We should eat them.

FARMER: Up all night barking...scratching my car....

WONG: Many people say dog meat has natural preventative and curative properties. We will post our recipes in homeopathic pharmacies as well.

FARMER: Terrorizing children... chasing people up the street...

When asked for more detail on his comments, Mr. Farmer was seen to compose himself a little more: "No one is in charge of these dogs. By my flat alone there are twenty. They seem bent on killing each other as well. B92 has set up a fund to protect them

– the Mila fund thing – but no one has set up a fund to protect us from the unnatural wild life of New Belgrade.

"If anyone laid a hand to them, they would be jailed immediately. We cannot count on the City to rid the neighborhoods of these wild dogs. We do not seem to have any kind animal shelter in working order. There is but one choice: Eat them.

"The menu at Psi will be set according to Grievance (this is a novelty I believe among restaurants). General annoyance will be cheap. But to get a chance to eat the dogs who scratched the paint off my Alfa Romeo incurring EUR 400 worth of damages, this will be premium priced cuisine. I suggest the Vietnamese Cho Xao Sa Ot. It is fried dog in lemon grass and chili. Very spicy indeed.

As a closing note, Messrs. Wong, Kim, Idibia, and Farmer would like to state that they have no plans of carving up family pets or beloved animals. But the ones left to be abandoned in the streets of New Belgrade, downgrading neighborhoods to third-world status, they will be served in abundance.

Before the restaurant opens its doors, it proprietors are waiting for a better solution to be proposed for these wild dogs. Write in care of Mila, B92.

Thank you.

Flex and Flexibility

Accused as I stand of a certain streak of inflexibility, I should like to say a few words on behalf of a little known attribute of human behavior which should, when properly applied, also serve to allow us to part company with the Great Apes along the Darwinian path.

I refer to The Plan.

I had always been under the impression that Planning, making plans, planning time, planning schedules and the like were part of what makes humans unique in the animal kingdom. Whereas the Grizzly does not sit down and draw up a list of things he will need for hibernation, we as humans would certainly have at least thought about it a few days before and set aside pyjamas, pillows, and blankets - maybe a good book, iPod, or small television – before setting our annual alarm clock and descending into torpor. The female of our species might have also included a few pairs of shoes, not knowing how the weather or necessity would be upon waking from the six-month sleep.

We make lists. We plan things ahead of time. We use phrases like "according to plan" or "make a plan" or "upsetting our plans." I always thought we LIKED planning.

An accumulation of years in the Balkans, however, has steadily and inexorably eroded this misconception and misinterpretation of Darwin.

What I have come to accept is that here we are drawn to the Perception of Planning. It is needed to show that we have an idea about what will happen next or what we plan to do tomorrow, the next day, and five years from now. But this is just for show. In reality, we have are Revolving Plans which get made *while we are already in motion.*

Just as I might say to myself that today I will wash the car, it is not really a Plan until I have been in the car and am moving in the proper direction for five minutes – moreover, not even really then unless the soap has been sprayed on already. Then, retrospectively, I will be able to pronounce that I both plan to wash the car and that I have achieved my objective.

Applause all around.

Today – getting back to my intransigent inflexibility – the Plan was to go see a baseball game at Ada. I had never done so before and therefore I attempted to plan it out: 1) last week I checked the schedule; 2) I informed my son to spark his anticipation; 3) we eschewed other possible plans for the long weekend to accommodate this; 4) mid-week, I RE-checked the schedule on Internet. But at the appointed time, the field of dreams on Ada was completely deserted. Nor were there any other disappointed fans milling about in disbelief. The schedule was published and was either a fiction or just a vague idea: in either case the upshot was the same. No baseball.

Now let's spot the errors. Points 1 through 4 were absolutely correct actions. But the error came BEFORE all this. I made the fatal mistake of making an actual plan. Everything I did was based on the erroneous assumption that Baseball would occur at the appointed time.

Sadly, when I saw the result, I was only slightly disappointed. This shows the extent to which the fatalism surrounding planning has infiltrated my brain. I shrugged it off (and people who know me will tell you that I am not often one for off-shrugging).

But later came the accusation of inflexibility. I planned to see this game and executed the plan (even if I was the only one). The friends who had also agreed to join us said I was inflexible because I stuck to the plan instead of changing it six times beforehand and ending up drinking coffee with them in Mercator. To them, I was inflexible because I did not allow the LATEST plan to override the ORIGINAL plan....

I protest this. We cannot be flexible at all unless we have a structure from which to make variations. If there are no plans, how can I alter them? And, in the absence of a better plan, why should I not keep the first one? Is life a picaresque novel in which one damn thing follows another without rhyme or reason? I don't want to accept this and therein lies my error.

Dear Readers, learn from my mistakes! Do not accept a plan as final when another one will come along! Learn to change plan at the drop of a hat! Practice dropping a few hats yourself! This way you will never be disappointed at a failed plan.

Or in the worst case, a frontal lobotomy would also work.

Calling the Guy

When something is broken in my immediate surroundings, I will call The Guy to come fix it.

This means the kitchen sink, the boiler, the fuse box, the electric outlets, the washing machine, the ripped shirt, the car, the window. Anything that we touch may break or cease to function at a moment's notice, whether or not I have struck it with a sledge hammer or tried to fill it with tomato juice. At that point, there is always someone out there whose special purpose in life is to repair the damage. We call the guy.

I say "we" call him, but more and more I am getting the impression that it is only me. Every time something goes wrong and I want to call the guy, I seem to get looks of sympathy and condescension. People (men in particular) think it is a personal failure if we cannot fix something ourselves but have to appeal to a mercenary 'majstor' to come in, assess the situation, shake his head sadly, and fix it in three minutes.

Today the Sink Guy came. I have had a leaky faucet for at least a year and finally I decided to call the plumber to come DO something about it. If I put my mind to it, bought forty different wrenches and spanners, I could spend about three days to remedy the leaky sink. I would wipe my brow in satisfaction of Good Job Well Done. And it would start its insidious dripping again in 48 hours. Instead, I called the Guy who fixed it immediately.

What's wrong with this?

It's like the man who cannot start his car. He will open the hood, stare vacantly inside the motor. He will tap a few metal things with a wrench, stand back with one hand on his hip, and when no one is looking, he will close it all down and call the mechanic. I estimate that about 80% of men know NOTHING about fixing cars. I also estimate that about 90% of that 80% will pretend to try to do it themselves first. I have no such grand delusions about my Inner Mechanic – he does not exist. So, being part of the 10% of the 80% and at the top of the 20% of the 100%, I call the Guy.

My psycho-social evaluation of this state of affairs plays out on two distinct levels: A) all guys think they should know how to fix everything; and, B) the importance of finger-pointing.

Point A. A large portion of male humans are born thinking that they can repair a short-circuit, fix a transmission, or replace a calcified thermostat. Moreover, an even larger portion is born thinking they could fix it BETTER than their next-door neighbor. It seems to be part of our genetic code, right there next to the hunting of mammoths and slaying of sabre-tooth tigers.

I am man. I hunt. I fix.

Point B. This part I think is far more determinant. It is very important to be able to effectively blame someone for a Bad Job Done Poorly. If you do it yourself and it does not work, you can always say: "What do I know? I studied philosophy and ontology! What's a gasket anyway?" On the other hand if you hire someone, you buy yourself an instant scapegoat. You can then say, with chest righteously puffed up: "That idiot! He had no idea! I will sue him!"

Which is more satisfying?

But in the end, you are *still* responsible as you *did* pay him for the work. You *did* choose him and you *did* engage him. The best solution is Secret Option C. You get your cousin to do it. Or you get a recommendation of a Guy to do it. Mostly these people will not charge you for the work (or not much) but then they become FULLY RESPONSIBLE for the bad job they did. You are not only able to point your finger at the Guy, but also at your friend/colleague/cousin/whoever who recommended the Guy.

Win-Win!

PASSING FANCIES

PASSING FANCIES

It's a bright and sunny day here in the White City on the Danube.
Daytime highs in the upper to mid-lowers and a chance of
collective participation is expected in the afternoon.
A great day to be out and about town.

Unless it snows. Then it sucks.

We like to talk about the weather. The weather ties us all together in one big bunch of grumbling cats in a bag. For a Grumpy Guy, the weather is a standby source of complaining. It's too hot. It's too wet. It's too cold. There are too many cows.

This section looks at some of these meteorological conditions which pain us, some of the passing thoughts and fancies which we might never have an occasion to think about otherwise. Holidays come and go. We change the hour twice a year and get confused every time. The world comes to an end (or threatens to) on a regular basis.

When it comes down to it, even humans will take a little time off from being generally incomprehensible, and we have to take a look at what the rest of the natural world is up to.

A little purple prose never hurt anyone – too much.

First Snow

Gently, the first snows wafting through the Belgrade skies, dispersing themselves randomly over the streets, the cars, the sleeping stray dogs, the three-wheeled gypsy bicycles, blanketing all indiscriminately. The first snows clothe the White City in ceremonial garb, in a winter dress uniform.

Uniform of perception, masking of distinction, the first snows are pristine. From the windows, children crane to see the white fields and folds of their landscape. Eyes widen, mouths slightly open. Sunless light, bright with reflection, traverses the glass panes and draws the first snows across parquets, tables, into our homes – no quarter is untouched, unaffected, unwhitened.

The whitened sepulchral shroud of winter is now laid out over the city. Silence reigns.

Under the first snows, Belgrade is Budapest, Bratislava, Sofia. Under the still clear snows, all disjointed parts integrate. Men in tuxedos, waiters and soldiers in uniform – individual distinctiveness pales and is subsumed in the greater, wider scope of vision.

All white. All vast. All one.

First snows evanescent. The white blanket is frail and erethreal. In moments, old features protrude, reemerge. Patches of brown and black multiply, leaving a tattered sheet of white to connect the shaded places. And the city returns. Harsh voices, metallic sounds, and atramental clouds billow again from snow-cleared cars.

The moment of the first snow blurs and fades into memory within the time it takes to perceive its luminous immensity.

First snow.

Wintering Up

Winter clothes. Summer clothes. Bags in, bags out. Sweaters, wool trousers, heavy suits, dark colors to absorb the watery winter sunlight. T-shirts, shorts, short sleeves. And do I really need this t-shirt that I could wear for the last time in the last century? Hm...

Sacks of discarded clothes: 1985, 1991, 1998, 2004, etc. All into heavy black bags and carted out to give to charity or family or whoever wants or might need them. Sacks of unusable clothes. How much STUFF can one person accumulate???

Winter tires. Insulation. When will this heat start working in the building? Winter jackets and coats. Scarves and gloves. And shouldn't I keep just one summer outfit in case? No. No! Out, away, packed, gone, banished, binned, burned, donated – get thee hence.

The ritual of the change in seasons, which happens twice a year in my home, involves the painful decisions about those items of clothes which I have not worn in decades but have not the heart to throw out. Two times in a year they are transferred from one bag to the other: maybe they will fit me next year. Maybe they will come back into fashion. And, of course, all of the clothes which should have been vanquished a long time ago must be pondered as well. Wide lapels, skinny ties, straight leg jeans, big collars, electric blue: did I *ever* wear this?

When I was a child, we used to do the biggest changeover in the spring, leading up to the Great Garage Sale. The Sale forced us to pick out and throw out and place a price of five cents on a priceless Led Zeppelin t-shirt. Although this was fun for kids, I can imagine the red- faced humiliation for the parents when people would browse by snickering and pointing at the ridiculous things accumulated in the house.

Like they had no fashion skeletons in their closets...

The winter conversion was always a little more melancholy. Wintering up meant the end of summer, back to school, no more playing all day long. Away went the uniforms of fun and out came the blue serge and grey flannel.

And now, we can sit and wait for the snow. The winterization is complete, done hurriedly after the temperature dropped from 30 to 3 in a day and a half. We sit in parkas and wool socks, in turtle necks and corduroy. The heat has come on in the building finally. In a week or two the clocks will change again and plunge us into winter darkness.

And the weather? Bright and summery on the way back: 25 degrees.

Sigh.

Statistics are Okay

I would like to be a ghost in Oklahoma.

I just discovered, quite by accident, a little town in Wagoner County, Oklahoma, called Okay. Okay, OK, has 597 people and a population density of 737.3 people per square mile. By my calculation, that makes 597 humans and 140.3 ghosts in a square mile.

As Okay, OK, does not actually have a square mile but rather only 0.8 square miles, it means that the extra 140 non-people (and the truncated 0.3) live on a space of about 518,000 square meters. For every fictional person or ghost in Okay, there are about 3700 square meters of space.

On that space, an ambitious ghost could build an office building, a few houses, and a small park with a slide, modern swing set, and jungle gym. I like the jungle gym idea as a ghost could never fall off it and break his arm.

What is all this about? It is about the numbers of course. It started out being about a town called Okay, OK, but the numbers attracted me more. Some group of dust bowl oldies sat around a checkerboard one day and decided to give their town a joke name. But the statisticians, serious folk in tweed with sophisticated machinery, are the ones who ran the numbers.

They came up with a mathematical expression of the population which relied on non- existent people for it to be entered in the records. Moreover the 597 people of Okay (fewer people than are milling about Mercator of a Saturday afternoon), the 2000 census broke them down into racial groups as well: 64.15% White, 4.36% African American, 21.27% Native American, 0.17% Asian, 0.50% Pacific Islander, 1.84% from other races, and 7.71% from two or more races. Hispanic or Latino of any race were 3.69% of the population.

One also wonders about the presence of 29 people from a Pacific island: why come to Okay?

And this is the point that rubs me wrong. Each of these percentage points are individuals, people, someone's mother, father, sister, brother, or much despised neighbor with a loud aggressive pit bull. They all have names – the delegation of 10 Asians presenting a pronunciation challenge for checkerboard contingent.

Statistics are ok as long as we are talking about large undefined groups. But as soon as the group is small enough for one guy to go out and count on a morning walk, it seems a little cold and inhuman to assign numerical values to them. As soon as you place a number instead of a name, you take away the stories which comprise their lives and leave them exposed to the cold unfeeling winds of demographics. Mr. Ng, who runs the hardware shop in Okay, OK, has a story. But as he constitutes only .017% of the population, his tale will certainly be overlooked. The Great 64% Majority will get all the press. The Wilsons, the Wainwrights, and the Joads. These are the Okies who inspired John Steinbeck. Their stories will be the ones we remember because they are a statistical majority.

But Mr. Ng has opinions. He has friends. He has neighbors. Mr. Ng may be a man of considerable influence on Main Street, Okay, OK. He may even be a trend setter. But we will never know this: Mr. Ng lives on the border between a statistical error and the great imaginary 140 people in the Okay Square Mile.

Let's talk to him before we start running the numbers on this town.

Appeal for Blueberries

Blueberry pie. Blueberry juice. Blueberry jam. Blueberry tarts. Blueberry preserves. Fresh blueberries. Frozen blueberries. Wild blueberries. Dried blueberries. Blueberry yoghurt. Blueberry barbeque sauce.

There are times when we accumulate so much information on a subject that it must needs burst forth and splat onto the page like squashed blueberry. The following is not a public service announcement or message. It is just overspill.

I discovered that blueberries will make you see better, will un-clog your arteries, and help you lose weight. Doctors even say it will help fight diseases and increase your memory. I started looking into this as a matter of course – I was working on a pro-ject. But I soon found out that I had become rather fascinated with the subject.

So, as a direct consequence which any self-diagnosed OCD suf-ferer will immediately understand, I sallied forth onto the pub-lic thoroughfare in search of these blueberry products. I have al-ways *liked* blueberries. I liked them in the way that people like any fruit – from time to time, generally *for* and generally not *against*, but not over-the-top and obsessive about it.

My thinking was that Serbia has a lot of fresh fruit production and blueberries were a goodly part of it. In fact, I discovered many blueberry products only here, even if the recollection of my grandmother's blueberry pie still brings a pang of nostalgia. So I expected to find a lot of blueberry stuff to buy and try and employ to anti-oxidize myself.

And yet…

I think I have been into every possible store where blueberries might be sold. I look for them; I ask for them. Most of the Fruit and Veg Professionals (the ones who have mastered the diffi-cult art of weighing food and stickering it) usually looked at me without answering. Some responses were:

No.

It's winter.

Ask my colleague.

What?

I finally located some at one Maxi shop, but they were on the edge of extinction by the time I got them home. I am still looking when I walk into grocery stores, but my hopes of finding them are diminishing.

Supply and demand is viscous. If I look and search and quest for blueberries and ultimately come up with an empty shopping basket, eventually I will start to lose interest (in my case it might take a few months) and then, in the end, I may stop altogether and forget about them. And if I stop looking and asking, shopkeepers will think I (i.e., the Consumer) could not be bothered about the blueberry. And they will not even think about stocking them.

In the meantime, no one takes stock of the amount of blueberry juice and jam and muffins which get sold every day and adduce thereupon that people actually LIKE blueberries.

But ok… What's the point? There is nothing unusual about all of this. Absolutely not. As I said before, this is overspill of information. But something about the blueberry and finding it and its benefits and taste remains with me. So I wanted to share it.

But since we do not have easy access to blueberries to enhance our memories, you can take comfort in the fact that you probably forget having read this appeal for blueberries a few minutes after closing the page.

Although you may find yourself craving some blueberry barbeque sauce…

Novak the Magnificent?

Let it come as to no one as a surprise to anyone: Novak Djoković did NOT walk on the moon.

Nor did he cure tuberculosis, invent the wheel, pave the Information Superhighway, or create the heavens and the earth in six days plus a day off to rest. To my knowledge, Mr. Djoković was not responsible for breaking down Apartheid, lifting the Iron Curtain, or debunking the weapons of mass destruction in Iraq.

He may, of course, have assassinated Bin Laden. No one knows quite WHAT happened there…

If you look at Belgrade over the last couple of days, however, you may come to wonder what he actually *did* do. He has been welcomed home from London as a hero, a national icon, someone of whom statues will surely be erected somewhere in Serbia, someone about whom elegies will be versified. The president, usurping as much of the spotlight as the cameras would allow, calls him a role model for the youth of Serbia.

(If I had a hat, I might remove it at this point.)

As it turns out, he won a lot of tennis. Tennis is a sport. A game, if you will. Certainly, it must be hard to win in a game which pits a lot of very good players against a lot of other very good players. I surely could not have done it, as any of my tennis partners would aver.

Moreover, many of the youth of Serbia to whom Novak the Super-Duper is a role model could not have done so either. This is notably, or so I am told, because the state does not allocate a lot of funds for individual sports such as tennis. We pay for basketball and football. Even water polo, I guess. In this way, I suppose the president is right: he is an example of how no one will help you until you are the world's number one and then they will try to take credit for it.

But let's be happy for Novak. After all, he did win. And he is the world number one for the moment. And let's be happy for ourselves too, since we live in the same country as he does. That must confer a little greatness on Serbia and, by extension, on the rest of us who live here.

After all, had he lost, he would have skulked into Nikola Tesla without fanfare, and it might have been just another Monday night in Belgrade. No kudos for second place here. Number Two is just number two.

I am aware that I shall not be making myself a lot of friends in my adopted homeland by nay-saying the apotheosis of Novak Djoković. But, really, enough already. No conversation in these last days has strayed far from his name. None will be clear of Novaks and Noles for at least a couple of weeks. And God help us all if he maintains the pace through Flushing Meadows. Yesterday evening, on the eve of the great victory, my son asked me if it was normal that people were riding on the top of their cars.

No, I said. It is not.

Skammdegisthunglyndi

In Iceland, they have a name for it.

It is the feeling of seasonal depression when the days start getting short and nights start coming sooner. "Skamm" means short, "degi" is day, "thung" is heavy and "lyndi" means mood.

Skammdegisthunglyndi

Until December 22, when the days start growing again, the occurrence of Short-Day- Heavy-Mood will be on the increase. In fact, we might well blame *everything* on it, as it seems to affect everyone to some extent. Get in a fight at the office? Skammdegisthunglyndi. Trouble at home? Skammdegisthunglyndi. Late to pay your electricity bill? Skammdegisthunglyndi.

Or just absent mindedness.

To some extent, we can blame the short days for the pandemic H1N1/09 virus (this is the official name, I found out, because "H1N1" is just the regular flu). One of the ways to avoid infection, apparently, is to get plenty of vitamin D. Since we get most of our vitamin D from sunlight, the short winter days are working against us. It is both unhealthy AND depressing.

Skammdegisthunglyndi.

For the global financial crisis, each day of depressed trading is even more depressing when you look out of the window at three in the afternoon and see only blackness. Employees, called into the manager's office for explanations might claim Skammdegisthunglyndi for their bad results. Managers, on the other hand, strolling around the office, may mistake the darkness for the end of the day and just leave. Skammdegis-**ljós**- lyndi?

"Ljós" means "light." I think I have just made this word up.

There is clearly much more to be said about this – to correlate productivity to the occurrence of Skammdegisthunglyndi, calculate the number of domestic squabbles, filibusters in parliament, and general grumpiness of the people in the days of darkness. Sadly, however, it is just after two in the afternoon and I should be going to sleep now.

Until spring.

How to Write Foreign Policy

First, you need a very large mixing bowl.

Take a generous helping of random opinions from diplomats around the world. To prepare this, send reasonably competent individuals to each country and marinate them in the local cultures for a few months. Be careful not to let them sit too long in the marinade or the local spices may overpower the flavor.

In the meantime, knead and stretch Basic Foreign Policy Objectives (available at most supermarkets in the frozen section) until they attain the shape which is best suitable to your baking dish. The choice of baking dishes is not always of great importance as you will only be half-baking your mixture anyway.

Into the bowl of random opinions, gently fold in mollifying agents at a ratio of 10:1. This will tend to homogenize the opinions and reduce the acidic taste which may be present in each individual ingredient.

TIP: Use a paste of conditional and subjunctive verbs and noncommittal adjectives.

For a spicier Foreign Policy, you may choose to add media commentary at this stage. Mix it in by hand, not with an electric mixer, as the commentary should be only fragmented enough as to remove its original context without disrupting its spirit or tone. Strain away any extraneous exclamation points or excessive question marks.

By this point, your mixture should resemble a thick grayish mush, like cold oatmeal or gruel. Do not be alarmed if it is unpalatable to the taste, the final outcome will be a Policy that lies just on the threshold between the gagging reflex and metabolic acidosis.

Pour the mush into the baking dish which you have lined with your unbendable Basic Foreign Policy Objective shell and bake at 3,500 degrees Kelvin for three and half seconds.

The result will melt your mixing bowl completely and petrify the shell without affecting the dyspeptic mush in the least.

Serve with a pinch of salt.

Precautions and Contraindications

Your Foreign Policy is now ready for general distribution and mass consumption. Most people to whom it is served will find it somewhat distasteful but will find themselves able to swallow it more or less readily. Digestion will be a very long process. The best Foreign Policies will never be fully digested at all.

Government chefs are warned of a new phenomenon which is affecting policy kitchens around the world. It is called Wikileaks.

Wikileaks is a *separating agent*. It removes the random opinions added in step one and serves them individually, without any mollifying agents, as completed dishes in and of themselves. This represents a danger to your Foreign Policy as it removes some of its bite, on the one side, and undermines the chef's intent on the other.

Served without sugar-coating, Wikileaks are often mistaken for the Real Thing. And very often people will find themselves filling up on the Wikileaks long before your Foreign Policy is served.

Be sure to warn your dinner guests appropriately beforehand

Think Purple

Purple cars and purple phones and purple plums. Smell the purple orchids and lisianthus. Breathe in the purple mountains and stand in purple rain. I am immersed in the deep purple that falls over sleepy garden walls.

Purple is amethyst and eggplant. It is indigo, lavender, lilac, mauve, mulberry, blueberry, orchid, plum, pomegranate, puce, royal, thistle, and violet.

Wine is not purple – but it makes me feel purple.

Purple sounds funny. Like grape soda popping between the lips. It is bubbly and serene. It is relaxation and royalty. And what about the "one-eyed one-horned flying purple people eater" – is it a people-eater that is purple? Or does it only eat purple people? It would often be quite hungry. The Joker has a purple suit, but his vest is green.

Purple is Milka and Cadbury Dairy Milk. It is Ralph Lauren's Purple Label. Yahoo! is purple and Crown Royal whiskey. Purple is the liturgical tone of Lent and Advent, the color of the crown chakra, and is the color of the plant Jupiter. Some people say Neptune is purple – some blue.

The purple poker chip is worth $5,000.

The Color Purple. The Purple Rose of Cairo. I never saw a Purple Cow. And Purple Haze, of course.

Soldiers get a Purple Heart for courage. The emperor of Byzantium signed his edicts in purple ink. Caesar Augustus declared that only the emperor could wear purple. And the Emperor was called "The Purple."

We can elaborate and write in purple prose, and the nobility is said to be born to the purple. When we have a purple patch, it means we are having good luck.

People say purple means good judgment, spirituality, and meditative mindsets. It is associated with magic, mystery, and Barney, the big purple dinosaur. It gives peace of mind and a sense of purpose. Purple indicates luxury, wealth, and sophistication. It is also feminine and romantic.

Dinl-Chi is purple in Navaho. *Pourpre* in French. And they call bishops "*la pourpre*". *Morado* in Spanish. *Porpora* in Italian. The Germans say *lila* after the flower. In Hindi it is

पपरुल (*parpala* but pronounced like "purple").

Purpleness, empurple, purpurate, purplish, violet, imperial, majestic, regal. The purple mombin is a tree, and no one lives in purple Chinese houses – they are flowers.

Purple perception. Think purple.

Hourless

We lose time when we sit and wait for the phone to ring. We lose time when watching the water boil for coffee and tea, looking for the keys, standing in queues. This blog will take me an hour to write – and where will that hour be tomorrow when I wake up and find that we have moved into summer time?

In the fall, when we gain an hour moving back into normal time, most of us use it to sleep. Either that, or we get up artificially early and say to ourselves that we have a much longer day in which to be Productive! But the change usually happens on Sunday so the extra hour is generally used in idleness…

The spring changeover makes us late for stuff. I have a plane to catch in the morning at 10:30 which is really only 9:30. What time should I set my alarm for? My mobile phone tends to change the hour automatically so if I compensate for the hour by setting it for an hour earlier, I will end up getting up at four in the morning. But what if my phone does not make the change? What if I am an hour late to get out the door? What if that taxi driver set his clock the wrong way?

Oh the headache of it all….

People claiming that they have been abducted by aliens say that time is lost, unaccounted for. Aliens generally do their abducting in normal times during the year so as not to cause confusion – never during the switch to summer time or winter time, never on February 29. It is just too messy.

Night people who will be up all night tonight working or playing, will find themselves physically unable to use that missing hour. Seeking ways to compensate, they may stay up later or start the night earlier, but the incontrovertible fact is that March 27 has only 23 hours in it. The 24th has been forfeited. Actually it is the third.

On an abstract level, when we think of time as a continuum, many questions are opened up. The events that happen from

02:01 to 02:59 on March 27, 2011 do not exist. Were there really events at all? If we consider that they actually happened on the reset clock between 03:01 and 03:59, how does it change the nature of the phenomenon? After all, when we measure space, we cannot omit the increment of physical space occurring between one and three meters – even if everyone agrees, it is still against the laws of physics. Two and half meters is NEVER three and a half meters, even if we all vote to say that it is.

Time, like space, is one of the seven fundamental physical quantities as defined by the metric system. Along with the others – length, mass, electric current, temperature, amount of substance, and luminous intensity – these units are considered objective, unchangeable, immutable. Why do we think we can mess around with time? Just because they do it all the time on Star Trek?

There is indeed more to say about this, but it will have to wait for October 30 this year, when I get my extra hour back.

Cows Around Town

We've all seen them. We pass by. We do not speak to them.

The cows around town, on Trg Republike, on Knez Mihajlova, generally mind their own business. They accost no one for theatre subscriptions, tissues, or wilted flowers. They do not ask the time or directions to Delta City. They look straight ahead into their forward progression or innocuously feed on the weeds growing from cracks in the paving. These are the Cows Around Town.

The Cows Around Town have been around. They have been in London, in Paris, in Rome. They are the brainchild of Walter Knapp and have purportedly grazed in hundreds of cities around the world since 1998. They call themselves the Cow Parade. But neither pomp nor ostentation follows in their wake. They are just cows of a different color. Not on parade, they are among us.

Some say they have appeared in Belgrade to show support for the ongoing farmer's strike. But the farmers have not discussed this. The cows are apolitical. They do not stand for office. They do not organize rallies. They do not even recognize the passing citizenry.

These are contemplative cows. They suffer themselves to be painted as tigers or splashed with incongruous colors. They bear up stoically under the children riding on their shoulders for photographic moments. They are neither proud nor are they ashamed. They assert their existence by merely existing.

In the deep of the night, the cows remain. They hold vigil even after the ever-earlier official closing of places of business or pleasure. They disturb no one (purposefully that is). They ask nothing of us. When dawn breaks again over the pedestrian walkway, they are there to greet the bleary-eyed and semi-conscious.

They do not judge.

We walk among them. We pass alongside them. We cast sidelong glances and pretend as though it is the most normal thing in the world to observe these Cows Around Town. They proliferate in quiet increments. As more cows appear, we shift our gait and our promenade to accommodate them. Will Belgrade soon be completely overrun with a serene bovine presence? The argument has been advanced that the cows were here in spirit before they had physicality.

But in the end, the Cows Around Town have been accepted and they accept us. We coexist peacefully. We have no expectations one of the other. We acknowledge that the space they occupy, in apposition with our own, is to be shared.

One could learn much from the Cows Around Town.

Dumbing It Down

I wonder if I know less today that the things which I have forgotten.

I used to remember phone numbers. I also remembered birthdays, street addresses, spelling, and peoples' names (although I was NEVER very good at that). Now I no longer need to remember. My phone holds ALL the phone numbers to which I have ever been exposed. It remembers for me. Street addresses are not nearly as relevant as email addresses – and email addresses are on their way to being completely supplanted by IM, Facebook, or chat identities.

Predictive spelling is pernicious and ubiquitous. I have to dig up the most arcane of vocabularies to be able to stump it. It completes my *thoughts* – not just my words – on the phone. Google is constantly asking me, "Did you mean…" and letting me know that Google understands my needs and desires better than I do.

And my thoughts! It occurs to me that my thoughts used to occur in full sentences and paragraphs, complete with punctuation, and that they used to formulate developed ideas or arguments. Today, my thoughts have been boiled down, condensed, and shriveled into bite-sized Status Updates. If I string enough of them together and throw in a few linking words (notwithstanding, however, although, and this-having-been-said), I may arrive at a paragraph of seemingly coherent non-random sentences.

This is not the ranting of a Grumpy Old Man against technology. No, rather it is an observation that I used to remember things that have by now been wiped clean from my cerebral cortex. Is it a BAD thing that I do not have to remember phone numbers? Not necessarily. In fact, although I used to remember a lot of numbers, there is no way that I could ever have hoped to know the thousands of names and numbers which populate my Outlook contacts.

This is Progress (capital P employed against the wishes of Windows spellchecking). We could say that Progress has allowed my memory to be expanded through technology. But we could just as easily say that Progress has actually *replaced* that same memory and left nothing in particular in its place. Progress and Technology (capital T, ditto) have not told me how I should use the extra space in my memory – it just provides the room.

More and more I notice that, in trying to remember a particular word, phrase, or name, I will willfully forego the use of the Internet, determined as I am to remember it all by myself, unaided by the omniscient collective mega-brains at Wikipedia, Google, and Dictionary dot com. The results are inconsistent, but when I do manage to extract the lost information from my head, it feels like a triumph of humanity over its creations.

I also notice that, since my memory seems to have a lot of leisure time at its disposal, that I remember myriad stupid things. I remember lyrics of songs that are now getting to be three decades old. I remember my phone number from 1972. I remember some of the birthdays which I used to know in the pre-technological era. I remember jingles from 1950s radio advertising which I heard as a child on compilations which I used to take from the library. I know what "LSMFT" means, for example.

Do we even use libraries anymore?

Do I think that humans are getting dumber? Do I think that the race is deprogramming its brains in order to evolve into giant bio-logical-organic processors? There is quite a bit of evidence to support the affirmative, but this is not the point. As with every inno-vative break-through, it usually takes several generations for hu-mans to catch up with their own ingenious tools. My children will know less than I did, but they will be infinitely smarter. And their children even more so.

My generation – the generation which spanned the chasm into the Information Age – works with a different operating system. We want to keep everything on our internal hard discs while new gen-erations are happy to deposit everything in the cloud. We continue to believe that what we learn and retain by dint of prodigious effort is MUCH more valuable than information which can be plucked like low-hanging fruit from a search engine. And if you ask me, we are right in so thinking.

But I should really check that on Google...

The End (Again)

The world as we know it ended seven months ago.

The world's legion paranoid masses announced the end of the world for May 21. I am not sure anymore why the world had to come to an end seven months ago, but it seems this month we will get another shot at putting our cosmic lives in order and getting ready for the New End of the World on December 21.

When the world ended seven months ago, none of us really noticed any changes. The next morning the sun seemed to shine, the birds seemed to sing. But since we had not yet reached the end of the 13th b'ak'tun of the Mayan calendar (which, as EVERYONE knows, is a really big deal), then the New and Real End of the World couldn't happen quite yet.

According to the sales, marketing, and advertising people with whom I have been conferring about 2012 phenomena in general, the December 21 deadline is likely to be postponed in order to stop consumers from boycotting their Christmas shopping.

Sales of the new 14th b'ak'tun calendar are available at www.the-world-is-not-really- going-to-end-just-yet.com. It looks a little like an Oreo cookie.

As it turns out, I already said my goodbyes to Planet Earth seven months ago. Since I am loath to repeat myself, I refer you to the previous Last Day of our mortal existence, in case you missed it in your bunkers and shelters.

As of this moment, we still have 20 days and a few hours before the Mayan calendar self-destructs and the world vanishes. But the clock is ticking. Before we all exit stage left, there are still a few things I would like to do, people I would like to see, and senseless memes I would like to share on Facebook. Knowing myself, I will waste at least three of my remaining days in composing a list of these things, another two prioritizing, and then the mad rush to get it all in before the appointed day.

I am keeping my calendar clear for the days following the end of the world. I think I will also engage a lawyer to work on the reckoning of my life on earth, just in case. The Post- Apocalyptic hourly rates will certainly go up prohibitively.

So this is goodbye – again. I am supposing that my current broadband account will no longer be valid in Oblivion, so my blog posts will almost certainly be less frequent.

That is, of course, unless the Mayans got it wrong.

The Second Thanksgiving

The Pilgrims, at Thanksgiving 1.0, were outnumbered almost two to one.

After washing up on Plymouth Rock in December of 1620, the 102 passengers of the Mayflower set about the task of conquering North America in the name of Puritanism. Religious fanaticism not being sufficient protection against Cold and Hunger, 46 of the original sinners died in the first winter.

With only 56 of them left, they enlisted the help of the Wampanoag to learn what to eat and how to grow it. It is said that the Wampanoag Nation had been fairly devastated by a bacterial outbreak of leptospirosis in the year or so preceding the English refugees' arrival, allowing English ships like the Mayflower to land nearly unopposed at someone else's house.

The first Thanksgiving, allegedly held in the autumn of 1621, was a three-day festival to which around 90 Wampanoags were invited alongside 56 of England's Least Desirables to celebrate the fact that they had not ALL died during the previous winter.

Over the next twenty plus years, up to 20,000 English escapees began to show up in modern-day Massachusetts and Rhode Island. Political and religious malcontents back home, unhappy with Catholic King Charles and not wanting to integrate into their own homeland, these Puritans then began to squabble and fight among themselves – shipping out the Quakers and other splinter groups preaching tolerance.

By the time we arrived at Thanksgiving 2.0 (55 years later in 1676), the following proclamation was made by Edward Rawson, Clerk of the Governing Council of Charleston, Massachusetts, before digging in:

"The Holy God having by a long and Continual Series of his Afflictive dispensations in and by the present Warr with the Heathen Natives of this land....

"The Council has thought meet to appoint and set apart the 29th day of this instant June, as a day of Solemn Thanksgiving and praise to God for such his Goodness and Favour, many Particulars of which mercy might be Instanced, but we doubt not those who are sensible of God's Afflictions...."

So, after half a century of afflictions (i.e. pesky native Wampanoags and disgruntled Puritans), the English invaders had something more to be thankful about again. This is a different dinner table from that of 1621 when they were so frighteningly outnumbered. Now there were thousands of English in Massachusetts and, packing muskets and other nifty tech from the old country, were able to push back the "Heathen Natives of this land".

And eventually they would kill most of them and cordon the rest off onto reservations.

As a note, there is much disagreement on the circumstances of the first thanksgiving and even as to whether it actually happened. But today, across the US and wherever Americans are settled, this is a day which remembers the pseudo-veracious story of the First Thanksgiving. The one before the cowering newbies had established dominion over the natives.

Thankful for surviving. Thankful for the bounty. And thankful for the backup that was on its way.

Negative Charge

Being gloomy, I have noted, makes you wise.

One of the things which I have yet to get my head around fully is the idea that negativity in Serbia is seen as a mark of intelligence, wisdom, and sagacity. And, by extension, being optimistic and upbeat makes people shake their collective heads and cluck their tongues.

Poor idiot, they say.

We are trained in this country to expect bad things. When something could work out well, it won't. When someone could be reasonable, he will not. When everything could come together nicely, it will all fall tragically apart. This is what we have come to expect, and this is how we should view the world. If we admit all this to ourselves, we will have achieved Wisdom. People will defer to our opinions. We will get quoted in newspapers, kafanas, and in corridors.

Random chance says this is wrong. The law of averages says the flip of the coin will come down both heads and tails equally over time. And by invoking this physical law, I came down on the side of the Idiots. Clearly I cannot possibly understand that random chance is NOT at work here. I must know that there are dark forces behind every fork in the road and that I will be pushed inexorably down a path to destruction if I take the risk of being optimistic.

A quick historical glance at Serbia proves them right. They see a violent history of upheaval, subjugation, conquest, and condescension and suddenly all their negativity seems justified. Anything that could go right will immediately go wrong because of the conspiracy of external forces which controls it. In this way, random chance does not stand a chance. It is all fixed.

Moreover, since there is nothing we can do about it, we tend to do things about it. We accept that the forces of negativity are holding the strings and, when faced with a problem, we act negatively. We complain. We yell and scream. We threaten and wave our fists in the air. By adding conflict, the outcome is then determined by the bigger fist. Between two men, one cannot always predict the outcome – but one will be hurt and the other victorious. Between Man and the System, the System always has the upper hand, and all our railing against it is for naught.

This vicious circle of negativity, however, is not unbreakable. Any average physicist will tell you that adding protons to a molecule with an excess of electrons will stabilize it. When (as happened to me this week) you are having a faceoff with a stubborn bureaucrat behind a window, a smile diffuses, a kind word can disarm.

Ok, I *watched* this happen while I was yelling and waving fists, but it is possible nevertheless.

I am caught in this circle just as much as anyone here. But I am also an Idiot. I continue to expect positive outcomes in difficult circumstances. I will always expect better and not worse. This leads me to a lot of disappointment a lot of the time, but it is also occasionally rewarded. The way I see it, if everything will end badly, then what is the point of doing anything?

Ah!

The point is that it is impossible for everything to end badly – some things do, some things don't. Heads or Tails. And even if the scales seem overbalanced on the negative side, it is only because the negative outcomes hurt us, and we remember them more. The fact is that the scales are scales. The law of averages has not been bought out by the forces of evil. They will mete out the good and bad evenly. In that case, why not expect the good?

Otherwise, we need not try anything at all.

How Things Should Be

I *do* like it here.

After so many years, it is still a question which I am asked repeatedly. *Do you like it here? Do you like living in Serbia?* Generally, I continue to answer affirmatively. The fact is that I am here, after having been here for quite a long time. And having no plans to move away, I guess I must like it here…

I am often criticized for writing about the things I find odd, strange, and unacceptable about Serbia. And I have very rarely shirked this self-assigned public duty to do so. So much of what happens around me runs contrary to my sense of How Things Should Be, a sense which has been developed and ingrained in me in many different places, different cultures, over many years.

The reality is that LIFE is full to overflowing with the odd, the strange, and the unacceptable. It is in every corner of the Earth, every city, and every home. Everywhere there are people who are different from you. And each time you meet them, something will strike an odd chord with you. At least it always does with me. It is not innately judgmental. It is a reaction to two colliding visions.

I have recently had the misfortune to read a blog post about Serbia in which the author – a foreigner – declares how he loves Serbia, Serbs, and does not want anything to change. My reading of that left me feeling rather dirty. His view was meant to be uplifting and positive and pro-Serbia. While the words were there, the feeling I got was that the entire country was being subjected to his condescending attitude. He looks down upon the people of this country and pats them on the head, showing how he feels that they are a little backward and primitive but essentially harmless.

Who is HE to say that?

There has long been a debate about the émigré and the immigrant. Many people are opposed to hosting unknown or different people in their country just because they are different. Perhaps they represent a threat, perhaps they are a menace. Or, more simply put, maybe they are just seen as a blight on an otherwise healthy society. This is usually the case when it is a question of large-scale immigration, including illegal residents.

From the standpoint of the émigré, the foreigner who has arrived in a country not his own in order to make a life for himself, it is a reductive vision. Most of what strikes us as unusual (or even wrong) comes from deep roots – things we learned as children in a different place, many hundreds or thousands of miles away. And such things *should* shock us – they are reminders of who we are and what we think. It does not imply that we are right or wrong, just that we know things differently.

I live here as a foreigner. I understand fully that I should not hope to be accepted as anything else. If you ask me if I like it here, I am more likely to tell you how long I have been here. If I tell you how much I LOVE it here, it would not ring true. If I tell you how much I HATE it here, you would be justified in telling me to leave. But the words themselves do not show anything. They may be true and sincere or hollow and false – there is no way to known which is the case except by observing actions over time.

So what *is* the way things should be? Things should be as they are. As should we all.

PASSING FANCIES

The Backword

It still happens to me.

I am walking down the street when someone will boldly approach me and ask if I am Chris Farmer. I am immediately put on Red Alert. Flashing lights in my mind are telling me that I have somehow offended him, or his mother, or his mother's neighbor, and that I will be asked to justify myself forthwith. But, after a period of wondering if my affairs are in order so I can meet my maker, I usually man up and admit that I am he.

On the street, and much to my relief, it usually goes fairly well. People just want to say hello, occasionally sign an autograph, or have a chat. Usually about my view on Novak Djoković since that inspired the most wrath of anything I have ever written in my life. This tendency does not stop the heart-attack-like symptoms each time however.

When I first arrived here, I was warned by [REDACTED] not to publish my name next to anything I wrote. There was a real fear that someone would read what I wrote, seek me out, and beat me to death with a clothes hanger. So at first I wrote under the pretentious pseudonym of "Odysseus".

But I soon tired of the wine-dark sea, the rosy-fingered dawn, and Circe and decided to use my own name. Yclept by my own moniker, I started in low gear. I tried to be inoffensive. I tried to play it down. I wanted to avoid the beatings and the clothes hangers. As time went by, however, a testing claw would be extended every now and then, until finally I decided it was safe enough to let loose the big dogs.

And this has not been without consequence. The twin pieces about Novak Djoković elicited a record number of responses from readers who asked me (in various degrees of politeness) to get out of here. Go home. Shut up. Take it back. A few of them wrote letters to Politika to get me fired. After three years of a monthly column, they finally listened...

Early on, I was threatened by JAT with a law suit about a piece I wrote (not in this volume) about being stranded in the fog in Timișoara. A former minister, who will remain nameless as long as he buys 100 copies of this book (*you know who you are...*), informed me through his staff that "my comments were not appreciated."

I have also had run-ins with readers who were determined to take my writings literally – that is, stripped of any irony. A discussion of the conditions in the Belgrade Zoo, for example, led me to say that the zoo could save money by stapling the bears to the wall instead of using cages. Let me be clear: this was IRONY.

I do not staple bears (unless I have no other choice).

It must be said, however, that on the whole my readers have been very generous. Many have remarked that I have sometimes pointed out something that they see every day and never thought it was strange. Being accosted by shopkeepers, making change, unmarked roads, parking violence, using the Cyrillic alphabet to advertise to foreigners...

And since the people in power take no notice of my commentary, I am pleased to note that Belgrade will continue to offer a wealth of subject matter to keep me writing well into my dotage. That should begin sometime tomorrow afternoon.

In closing, I would like to thank the politicians, the kiosk owners, the Sunday drivers, the shopkeepers and salesclerks, the medical profession, the urban planners, the ćevapi-sellers, the café-goers, the marketeers, and everyone else who has contributed to my loopy-eyed view of Belgrade. Please keep doing what you do!

And I will continue to be confused and grumpy.